GRAND RAPIDS
AND THE
CIVIL WAR

ROGER L. ROSENTRETER

THE
History
PRESS

Published by The History Press
Charleston, SC
www.historypress.com

Copyright © 2018 by Roger L. Rosentreter
All rights reserved

First published 2018

Manufactured in the United States

ISBN 9781467119191

Library of Congress Control Number: 2017963230

CONTENTS

Dedicated to the Grand Rapids Civil War Round Table

ACKNOWLEDGEMENTS

Christmas, tax day, birthdays, a wedding anniversary or a doctor's check-up are among our most important annual events. I would add my yearly presentation to the Grand Rapids Civil War Round Table. This standing invitation, which began many years ago, has greatly expanded my knowledge of Michigan and the war and is much appreciated.

My fourth grade teacher gets credit for sparking my initial interest in the Civil War. It was the early 1960s, and I wrote every Civil War centennial organization, pleading with them to send me all their "free stuff." (I still have those materials.) College later offered me opportunities to study under Western Michigan University professor Albert Castel (a respected Civil War author) and Michigan State University professor Frederick D. Williams (a member of the Michigan Civil War Centennial Observance Commission). Both scholars furthered my Civil War interest and knowledge. With my college days behind me, Paul Mehney (my assistant editor at *Michigan History* magazine) introduced the fascinating world of Civil War artifact collecting, as well as reenacting (albeit the latter on only one memorable occasion). Since the early 1990s, teaching the Civil War course for MSU's History Department allowed me to continue studying the conflict while sharing it with hundreds of undergraduates. Finally, my years at *Michigan History* magazine presented opportunities to author an occasional article about Michiganians in the war. However, *Grand Rapids and the Civil War* is my first Civil War book-length effort.

As the state's second-largest city in 1861, Grand Rapids (and the surrounding towns in Kent County) sent more than four thousand soldiers to war—5 percent of the state's "boys in blue." Significant wartime accomplishments included helping Michigan earn a distinguished cavalier reputation, providing the architects of one of the most unique units and sending to war a dentist who entered as a captain and emerged four years later as a brevet major general. Finally, diary entries and select letters from Valley City women offer a valuable glimpse of the oft-overlooked homefront.

As all authors know, writing is not a solitary endeavor.

Dr. Le Roy Barnett (retired State of Michigan archivist), Dr. Samuel Thomas (MSU History Professor Emeritus) and copyeditor Ann Weller offered much-appreciated contributions and corrections to this endeavor.

The book's images are greatly enhanced thanks to Dave Broene (Grand Rapids Civil War collector), Jennifer Andrew (Grand Rapids Public Library), Jessica Harden (State Archives of Michigan) and Bill Harrison (Custom Photo), who performed his usual magic cleaning up several of the images.

At The History Press, commissioning editor Ben Gibson kept me focused on getting the job done, while production editor Abigail Fleming corrected stylistic errors and led me through some of the minefields of recent trends in publishing.

It was a pleasant and rewarding experience working with all of these professionals.

Last, but not least, a special thanks to my "coach," Lisa, and our ever-faithful four-legged buddy Louis (among the most devoted editorial assistants in my experience).

ROGER L. ROSENTRETER
Okemos, Michigan

1

OFF TO WAR

Private opinions and private feelings must give way to duty when war exists. And it is our duty and that of every patriot[ic] citizen to adhere to his loyalty and uphold his country's flag….Politics may go to the shades, till the fight is over.
—Grand Rapids Enquirer, *April 20, 1861*

The guns had hardly cooled in Charleston Harbor when northerners enthusiastically responded to President Abraham Lincoln's call to put down an insurrection in the southern states. In Grand Rapids, the response "was prompt, and the rush to arms instantaneous." On April 15, 1861, an overflowing crowd possessing "a spirit of intense patriotism" jammed into Luce Hall. Built in 1856 at the corner of Monroe and Ottawa Streets, Luce Hall was named for wealthy businessman Ransom C. Luce and accommodated about one thousand people. Mexican War veteran Andrew T. McReynolds, the first of several speakers, wondered if the North would "tamely stand by and endure the insults and outrages" of Southern Rebels. The assemblage offered a resounding "no." The Reverend Stephen S.N. Greeley, pastor of the city's First Congregational Church, underscored what the nation needed was "patriotism, not partisanship." Vowing that the Old Northwest Territory "had always been in favor of freedom and human rights," Greeley guaranteed the North would respond to "this contest with vigor and alacrity." George Gray, a future cavalry commandant, struck an even harsher tone. Time for talking had passed, the Grand Rapids lawyer declared. The South "had violated the laws," and he predicted Valley

City residents "would arm themselves to a man" and support the nation's honor and its armies. Following the speeches, the citizens charged that the "unprovoked attack" on Fort Sumter merited "the severest punishment which the government can inflict." The citizens also confirmed their veneration for the Constitution and promised to stand with President Lincoln in "every attempt to put down the rebellion [and] to punish treason."[1]

Less than a week after this initial meeting, Grand Rapids residents, both men and women, "rammed, jammed and crammed Luce Hall once again. The singing of patriotic songs (including one titled "Our Union, Right or Wrong") followed several speakers. On Saturday, April 27, residents gathered once again for another patriotic display. Businesses were closed during the afternoon, and the Stars and Stripes flew from many homes and stores. The Reverend Courtney Smith of the First Presbyterian Church opened the festivities with a prayer, followed by the raising of the Stars and Stripes and a thirteen-gun salute. Former mayor Thomas B. Church offered an "earnest" declaration, while Republican congressman Francis Kellogg won plaudits from a Democratic rival for his "usual earnest and effective style." The city's fire companies and militia companies marched up Fulton Street to the city square, while Ada Webb won accolades for singing a song specially written for the gathering that expressed "the most unflinching patriotic ideas." The festivities ended with everyone taking an oath of allegiance to the United States.[2]

Despite a generally passionate response to the coming of war, some voices urged restraint in the days following Fort Sumter's surrender. The *Grand Rapids Enquirer*, the city's Democratic newspaper, warned against the growth of "war fever." While the paper acknowledged "the dignity of the nation should never be offended with impunity, and its flag should never be lowered without resistance," it blamed men from "both sections" for violating the Constitution and bringing on bloodshed. Guilty Northerners, in the opinion of the partisan *Enquirer*, were Republicans. The "prevailing war spirit" needed to be halted, or the nation was headed toward "disaster and distress." If Northerners resisted and discouraged the war feeling "so industriously activated by fanatics," the *Enquirer* reasoned, the Lincoln government would "speedily" change its tone. Despite its warnings and accusations, the *Enquirer* walked a narrow line in April 1861, making sure to avoid being labeled traitorous. It supported the growing Northern war effort but promised to keep reminding Republicans the impending conflict was their fault. The Democrat newspaper conceded that the government "must be sustained" but urged

John Mann, Thomas Mitchell, Charles F. Kendall and Joseph Herkner (*left to right*) belonged to the Grand Rapids Greys, one of the city's four militia companies. All four men served in different units; Mitchell died of wounds received at the Battle of Stones River. *Courtesy of Grand Rapids Public Library.*

the war effort be shaped by "an influence of kindness, of conciliation and forbearance toward southerners."[3]

After the initial shock and outrage over the attack on Fort Sumter passed, Grand Rapids turned its attention to preparing men to go to war. Within a few days of the president's call for troops, citizens gathered at the armory of the Valley City Guards—hailed as the city's "finest" militia company—and laid the foundation for the Third Michigan Volunteer Infantry Regiment.[4]

Camp Anderson served as the city's military epicenter during the war's early days. Located on the south side, about one and a half miles from the business center at Monroe and Canal Streets, the camp was "a veritable bee-hive of busy preparation" during the month of May. According to one contemporary observer, Grand Rapids could not offer "a more delightful spot for the purposes of a military display." The impromptu training facility possessed an exceptional parade ground, a large grove of trees and plenty of good drinking water. Enlistees with carpentry skills constructed additional structures, eliminating a shortage of barracks. Despite "the mud, rain, and mist," the camp's dedication ceremonies featured music by the regimental band, led by drum major Valentine Rebhun, a German immigrant and skilled percussionist. On occasion, local citizens visited the camp and watched the men drilling. Rebecca Richmond, a twenty-year-old socialite, recorded, "The [camp] fire in a grove of trees, with the smoke curling gracefully, produced a beautiful effect....The gleam of the arms, stacked around the fire, gave a slight martial tone to the scene, making it, however, none the less romantic."[5]

In late May, uniforms and equipment began arriving at Camp Anderson. Lewis Porter, who operated the city's oldest clothing store, provided the uniforms, and a Detroit firm produced one thousand pairs of brogans (shoes). As soon as the men had their uniforms, the Third Michigan held a dress parade, and observers noted how impressive the men

Twenty-year-old Rebecca Richmond assumed a leading role as Grand Rapids sent the Third Michigan Infantry off to war in June 1861. *Courtesy of Grand Rapids Public Library.*

looked. The uniforms—the first clean clothes the men had been issued in several weeks—understandably enhanced the soldiers' pride.[6]

Five of the ten companies in the Third Michigan Infantry had solid Grand Rapids roots, as did the regiment's field officers. Thirty-three-year-old Daniel McConnell was appointed colonel. An English native who came to the United States at the age of five, McConnell had served sixteen months of active duty with the U.S. Army during the Mexican War. He and his wife (from Ann Arbor) moved to Grand Rapids in 1849, and he entered the mercantile business and joined the Valley City Guards. After a two-year hiatus in California (presumably looking for gold), McConnell returned to Grand Rapids empty-handed. The regiment's lieutenant colonel was thirty-two-year-old Ambrose A. Stevens, a native New Yorker who had moved to Ionia in 1856. Major Samuel G. Champlin, a prominent thirty-four-year-old Kent County lawyer, judge and prosecutor, also organized the regiment's Company F. Edward S. Earle, a thirty-one-year-old veteran of New York City's famed Seventh Regiment before moving west, enlisted as adjutant. Quartermaster Robert M. Collins, also from the Valley City Guards, possessed a character "unsullied for probity and high moral worth." The Reverend Francis H. Cuming, hailed as a Grand Rapids institution, provided the regiment's religious guidance. A Connecticut native, the Reverend Cuming arrived in the Valley City in 1843. Under Cuming's "devoted and energetic" leadership, St. Mark's Episcopal Church expanded to more than three hundred members and built an impressive new building on Prospect Hill. The regiment's medical team consisted of two New York brothers, Dr. Willard Bliss (surgeon) and Zenas E. Bliss (assistant surgeon). The elder of the two, Dr. Willard Bliss earned his medical degree from Case Western Reserve College (class of 1845) and arrived in Grand Rapids in 1854, "where he quickly took position in the front rank in his profession." The younger Bliss received his medical degree from the University of Michigan in 1855 and practiced in Ionia until the outbreak of the war.[7]

As the men prepared to go to war, Grand Rapids women did not remain idle. Ten days after the fall of Fort Sumter, the Reverend Greeley's wife presided over a meeting that led to the organization of the Grand Rapids Soldiers' Aid Society. As the *Grand Rapids Enquirer* explained, the women were mindful "of the perils which threaten our country" and appreciated the patriotism shown by their menfolk "to take to the field in defense of the Flag of our Union." They promised to "cheer and heroically encourage [the] volunteers to brave every danger, encounter manfully every conflict, and overcome every obstacle in the path of duty." For soldiers who fell in

Among the best known Grand Rapids physicians, Dr. D. Willard Bliss served the entire war, first as surgeon of the Third Michigan Infantry, then as superintendent of one of the major hospitals in Washington, D.C. Dr. Bliss's younger brother, Zenas, also served the Third Michigan as surgeon. *From Baxter,* History of the City of Grand Rapids, Michigan.

battle, the society vowed, "their memories shall ever be cherished in our hearts, and the families of such shall never want for friends and support in time of need."[8]

The women mustered their sewing skills, making "housewives" (sewing kits), havelocks (a cloth cover placed over the kepi, a sort of cap, to protect the neck from the sun) and other necessities. Within a few weeks, an observer who visited one location discovered eight to ten sewing machines "in active operation." To spread their message wide and clear, the women created a committee to recruit additional volunteers. The women held daily meetings and, as one participant recorded in her diary, "attendance is good, and much work is accomplished."[9]

The women also devoted their attention to making the colors for the Third Michigan Infantry. Despite the city's display of intense patriotism, soliciting contributions for the regimental flag proved challenging. One woman grumbled how she spent two hours raising a mere three dollars, often hearing the "universal cry [of] 'hard times'" as an excuse for making only a small monetary contribution. But the women were not dissuaded. Their final product was six-foot square made of blue silk with heavy yellow fringe. On the front, embroidered in "corn-colored silk," was the U.S. coat of arms with the words "Volunteers, Third Regiment, Mich." On the obverse, the same coat of arms was accompanied by the words "The Ladies of Grand Rapids to the Third Michigan Infantry." Observers particularly noted the beautiful embroidery work of Maggie Ferguson. The flag was placed on a mahogany pike with a gilt spearhead and silken tassels.[10]

Daniel Littlefield of Grand Rapids entered the Third Michigan Infantry as a corporal in June 1861. In late 1862, he transferred to the Seventh Michigan Cavalry, rising in rank to first lieutenant. Littlefield did not survive the war, dying of disease at Washington, D.C., in early 1864. *Courtesy of Grand Rapids Public Library*.

On Monday, June 3, the Grand Rapids ladies arrived at Camp Anderson to present the Third Michigan with the regimental colors and various personal items. Led by a brass band, a long procession estimated at four thousand persons entered the camp. Colonel McReynolds and the Reverend Cuming offered brief remarks, which were followed by the singing of "The Star-Spangled Banner." Six young ladies, wearing "blue dresses with sashes of red and white confined on the right shoulder by a star [and carrying] blue parasols…[with] a cluster of 13 small gilt stars," presented the colors to Colonel McConnell, who immediately transferred them to the regiment's color company. Company commanders escorted the girls, each wearing "red Zouave jackets and brown jockey hats trimmed with red, white, and blue," to distribute Bibles, housewives and havelocks to the men. Captains also received bouquets of flowers. The Reverend Cuming closed the day with a prayer and benediction. When the festivities ended, the soldiers cheered the ladies of Grand Rapids and their new flag. Rebecca Richmond, one of the ceremony's participants, entered into her diary that she was "fatigued, but pleased and satisfied." Undoubtedly sentiments felt by many that day.[11]

Besides flowers and flags, the Third Michigan also received orders from the War Department to depart immediately for Washington, D.C. The day after mustering into federal service on June 11, the regiment held a dress parade. Rebecca chronicled what she saw next:

> *When the men were disbanded they seemed perfectly wild with excitement, congratulating one another in the most hearty manner, cheering and singing. Many of them immediately brought forth from the barracks their bundles containing worldly effects, and proceeded joyfully to packing their backpacks.*

As the regiment packed in preparation of leaving, local citizens formed a Third Michigan Aid Society to help the soldiers' families deal with future needs.[12]

Before dawn on June 13, the Third Michigan camp bustled with activity. One observer noted, "The Sergeants were supervising the packing and transportation of the baggage; the musicians were brightening up their instruments; the fifers were fifing; the drummers were drumming; the commissioned officers were forming their men into companies." With flags flying "everywhere," local firemen led the Third Michigan and "a vast procession of carriages" to the train depot amid "a continual ovation." Young girls showered the men with flowers as an estimated fifteen thousand people (twice the city's population) cheered and waved handkerchiefs. It "was an exciting time for many of the boys," one soldier recorded. Relatives and friends lined the whole route or "marched alongside their brave soldier boys." However, not everyone was joyous. Captain Edwin S. Pierce of Lyons (Company E) had

At the outbreak of the war, twenty-nine-year-old Benjamin C. Tracy of Grand Rapids joined the Third Michigan Infantry as a sergeant. He rose in the ranks to first lieutenant and ended his wartime service as brigade quartermaster in June 1864. *Courtesy of the State Archives of Michigan.*

"tearful eyes" as he bid farewell to his bride of two days. (Pierce survived the war and returned to his wife, Mary Chamberlain Pierce of Grand Rapids.) As the men boarded two trains of ten cars each, they received more flowers. Amid more hurrahs and waving handkerchiefs, the Third Michigan Infantry headed to war.[13]

After the trains had departed, a calmer Grand Rapids pondered the future. Boasting that the Third Michigan was "superior" to the state's two volunteer regiments already in service, the *Grand Rapids Enquirer* hoped the men would come home unharmed. "But if, in the common fate of battle, some shall fall," the newspaper contemplated, "we know it will be with their faces to the enemy. They are a noble set of fellows, and we shall not see their likes again." At the same time, socialite Rebecca Richmond bemoaned in her diary, "I can't help thinking how dull, quiet and sad it will be in Grand Rapids this summer!" Both were wrong. The departure of the city's "pet regiment," as Rebecca called the Third Michigan, did not dampen the city's patriotic ardor. Instead, a determination to defend the Union cause "grew stronger and more intense as the conflict deepened."[14]

2

THE CITY THEY LEFT BEHIND

The country is settling very fast with respectable inhabitants…of the most intelligent, enterprising and industrious character.
—*Joel Guild, Grand Rapids pioneer, December 1833*

When the men of the Third Michigan Infantry Regiment headed to Washington in early June 1861, they left behind a hometown fulfilling an early pioneer's prediction that the area "would one day become a place of great importance."[15]

The Grand River rapids that gave the city its name had attracted Native Americans as early as 500 BC. In the late eighteenth century, fur traders moved through the area, and in the mid-1820s, Isaac McCoy, a Baptist missionary, established a mission to Christianize Odawa Indians who lived along the river. A few years after McCoy's mission opened, Louis Campau and Lucius Lyon both contributed to establishing a settlement along the rapids. A Detroit native, Campau arrived in 1827 and founded a fur-trading post in the city's future central business district. Campau's operation grew into a "thriving" enterprise, aided by the arrival of his three brothers. A Vermont native who arrived in Michigan in 1821, Lucius Lyon surveyed the Michigan Territory before being elected one of its first U.S. senators. Campau and Lyon purchased land on opposite sides of the river and feuded over platting the area. Lyon named his settlement Kent; Campau chose Grand Rapids. Lyon, whose many commitments elsewhere minimized his influence in this matter, could

A native of Massachusetts, Thomas B. Church settled in Grand Rapids twenty years before the Civil War. Having studied law at Harvard College, Church served Grand Rapids in a variety of "representative positions of public trust and responsibility," including a term as the city's mayor. Well read in the classics and noted for his height, Church often gave orations at public gatherings like Independence Day. His son Fred served with an Illinois battery. *Courtesy of Grand Rapids Public Library.*

take some solace in the county being named after James Kent, a New York legal scholar.[16]

Settlers began arriving at Grand Rapids during the 1830s—a period known as "the years of occupation." Joel Guild and his wife and daughters were among the earliest pioneers. In December 1833, Guild boasted to friends back in New York that he had purchased 120 acres "of first rate land" and two lots in the newly platted village. "People are flocking in from all parts," Guild bragged. "The country is settling very fast with respectable inhabitants." In April 1837, the *Grand River Times*, the settlement's first newspaper, offered an enthusiastic appraisal of early Grand Rapids. If the area's natural beauty, rich soil, clean water and numerous employment opportunities did not offer enough good reasons to settle in Grand Rapids, the early pioneers were "of the most intelligent, enterprising and industrious character." Soon after the Kent County courthouse opened in the newly incorporated village of Grand Rapids in 1838, Lucius Lyon boasted in a lengthy letter to the editor of the *New York Herald*, "Michigan is the Garden of the Great West and the Grand River Valley is the garden of Michigan."[17]

Although Grand Rapids experienced "steady, though not very rapid, growth" during the 1840s, that changed considerably during the 1850s. Voters adopted a city charter in 1850, and a few years later, a plank road connected Grand Rapids with Kalamazoo. In 1858, an enthusiastic Mayor G.M. McGray celebrated the arrival of the telegraph linking his city with Detroit. (McGray described the telegraph as "that mysterious agent which

A view of
Ottawa
Street, 1865.
*Courtesy of
Grand Rapids
Public Library.*

makes all nations one and mankind a brotherhood.") In the same year, the
arrival of the first railroad led to a day "of big considerable rejoicing."
During the late 1850s, Grand Rapids also witnessed "great and expensive
changes and improvement," including the introduction of a new luxury—
gas streetlights.[18]

Even setbacks only proved a temporary hindrance. On the evening of
April 5, 1858, residents beheld "a dazzling sight" when flames engulfed
the eight-hundred-foot-long shingled-roof bridge across the Grand River.
A footbridge and a ferry provided a temporary river crossing until a new
bridge opened later that year. An even more devastating fire on January
23, 1860, destroyed public papers, most notably many of the city's real
estate documents. Despite the loss of these irreplaceable records, lawyers
agreed not to take advantage in litigation but promised to work "as much as
possible" in mutually using the surviving documents.[19]

Notwithstanding the threatening war clouds and lingering effects of
the 1857 depression, Grand Rapids experienced "a new spur to business,
which from that time grew greatly in volume and importance, and for
many years added to the local and general prosperity." In 1850, the city
recorded a population of 2,686 people, leading an eastern correspondent
to predict that "in a few years," the city would boast 10,000 residents and
rank as the state's second leading city. He was close. The 1860 census
counted 8,090 people in Grand Rapids, making it the state's second most
populous city.[20]

The Third Michigan Goes to War

I used to think it foolishness to dodge a cannonball but I think the other way now.
—Sergeant George W. Miller, Third Michigan Infantry

When word reached Grand Rapids about the Union setback at Bull Run, Rebecca Richmond confided in her diary, "The defeat, being so entirely unlooked for, startled and confounded us." Many Northerners shared similar feelings over losing the war's first big battle, but they hunkered down and prepared for a long war more determined than ever.[21]

The Third Michigan Infantry Regiment arrived in the nation's capital on June 16, 1861. Less than one month later, it was part of the inexperienced Union army trudging along toward a place called Manassas to confront an equally untried Rebel army. The Third Michigan belonged to a brigade commanded by Colonel Isaac Richardson, a West Pointer from Pontiac, Michigan. At a ford called Blackburn's on a stream named Bull Run, the two armies clashed on July 18. George W. Miller, a nineteen-year-old from Kent County's Bowne Township, was among the novice soldiers on the field that day. A member of Captain Samuel A. Judd's Company A, Miller shared the day's experiences with his parents. "We were taken into an open field where we made excellent marks for the enemy who commenced firing at us, but fortunately not a man was hurt." A skilled marksman soon promoted to sergeant, Miller also was "a lively writer," despite little formal education. Later on that warm July day, the Third pulled back from its exposed position. But as gunners exchanged artillery salvos, Miller conceded, "I

The earliest enlistees in the Third Michigan Infantry included (*left to right*) John Shaw, Chandler Andrew, Benjamin Gardner, Herman Kusig and James C. Jones. Gardner was from Kent County and survived the war unscathed, mustering out at the end of his three-year enlistment. *Courtesy of Dave Broene.*

used to think it foolishness to dodge a cannonball but I think the other way now." He told his parents, "You can hear a cannonball quite a while before it gets to you and sometimes you can see them. I saw several that were coming pretty strate [*sic*] for us in time to dodge them." Three days later, Richardson's brigade covered the routed Union army as it fled back to Washington, D.C. Colonel Richardson later commended the Third for being among the first Union troops to engage the enemy at Bull Run and for demonstrating "coolness and order" in covering the Yankee retreat.[22]

In the months following the Battle of First Bull Run, the Third Michigan occupied camps around the nation's capital. George Miller described it as "the laziest life" he had ever seen. "It is like a continuation of Sundays," he admitted. The Third was part of the rapidly growing Army of the Potomac, commanded by the North's new military sensation, General George McClellan. Like many of his fellow soldiers, Miller admired McClellan even as the workload intensified. After weeks of drilling, Miller boasted he could march twice as far as he could "at first," all the while carrying a thirty-pound pack, his rifle and forty rounds of ammunition. Despite grand reviews involving tens of thousands of men (and with the occasional visit by President Lincoln), Miller grew increasingly bored. In late January 1862, he

Left: Joseph R. Brown from Ottawa County enlisted in the Third Michigan Infantry shortly after the Rebel bombardment of Fort Sumter. At the Second Battle of Bull Run, the thirty-five-year-old Brown was seriously wounded. He survived but lost his leg to amputation. *Courtesy of Dave Broene.*

Right: An early recruit of the Third Michigan Infantry, Reuben Randall Jr. of Ottawa County was wounded at the Battle of Fair Oaks and later discharged for disability. *Courtesy Dave of Broene.*

agonized, "Times are awful dull here....I hope this war will end soon. I am sick of laying around and playing soldier for nothing."[23]

Miller's boredom soon ended. In late March 1862, the Army of the Potomac undertook an ambitious and unorthodox campaign to flank the Rebel army by moving up Virginia's York Peninsula. As the northern army inched its way toward the Confederate capital, Miller admired the "splendid country" and boasted, "We will soon be in Richmond." Campaigning also exposed the men to some of the real horrors of war. Following an exchange of gunfire, the Third Michigan occupied a Rebel position strewn with enemy dead. "It looks rather rough to see so many dead men," but Miller reasoned that "a soldier soon learns to look at these things as a matter of course." He swelled with pride when a captured Rebel admitted he and his comrades ran away after realizing they were fighting the "blue devils" from the Midwest.[24]

The Yankee advance abruptly halted a few miles from Richmond when the Rebel army attacked. The Battle of Fair Oaks, fought on May 31 and June 1, 1862, left the Third Michigan bloodied and counting losses of 30 killed, 124 wounded and 15 missing. Among the dead was Captain Samuel Judd, a man who the *Grand Rapids Enquirer* noted was "universally respected" by all of Grand Rapids. Judd's death led the city's firemen to adopt resolutions acknowledging the "untimely death of our late friend and brother…an excellent citizen, a brave soldier, and a true-hearted fireman, whose noble qualities of head and heart endeared him to all who were so fortunate to know him." Understandably, the city held a large funeral with the Reverend Stephen S.N. Greeley presiding. Others wounded at Fair Oaks included Colonel Stephen Champlin and Sergeant George E. Judd, Captain Judd's brother, whose shattered arm required amputation. (Judd returned to service, finally leaving the army as a captain in 1870.) Sergeant George Miller was among the missing, and hopes that he had been captured soon faded. Miller's remains were never identified, although he has a tombstone

Captain Samuel A. Judd, pictured here with his wife and children, mustered with the Third Michigan Infantry in June 1861. Commanding Company A, the twenty-eight-year-old Judd was killed at the Battle of Fair Oaks, which led to a citywide outpouring of grief for a "universally respected" soldier. In the same battle, Sergeant George Judd, the captain's younger brother, also fell severely wounded. *Courtesy of Grand Rapids Public Library.*

Twenty-year-old John Hanna enlisted in the Third Michigan Infantry on March 18, 1862. At Hatcher's Run, Virginia, on October 27, 1864, Hanna was wounded and taken prisoner. *Courtesy of Dave Broene.*

in the family plot at the Bowne Township cemetery. When word reached Grand Rapids of the losses at Fair Oaks, the city held "short and sad services" at the First Congregational Church. Rebecca Richmond confided in her diary, "Our city is in a state of excitement and mourning and constantly expecting and dreading a confirmation of our worst fears." Shortly after the battle, the regiment's officers met and adopted a series of resolutions expressing admiration for those who fell and consoling their loved ones back home. As the officers resolved, "Southern chivalry was unable to compete with Northern valor."[25]

In mid-August, the Army of the Potomac retreated following its unsuccessful Peninsula Campaign. Within a few days, the Third Michigan suffered heavy losses at the Second Battle of Bull Run. Colonel Champlin, who returned even though his severe Fair Oaks wound had not completely healed, was disabled. The losses worsened when the Michiganians were victims of "friendly fire." As one veteran described, with Rebels on the left and front and Pennsylvanians firing "on us from behind," the battlefield was "a horrid place." The regiment's national flag was "shot to bits…until there was not a piece as big as your left hand." The state colors "fared but little better." The Third Michigan went into battle with 260 men present for duty. It suffered 23 killed, 100 wounded and 16 missing. After Second Bull Run, Lieutenant Colonel Byron R. Pierce assumed command of the Third.[26]

BYRON ROOT PIERCE

Byron R. Pierce came to Grand Rapids from his native New York in 1856, taking up the profession of dentistry. He served as a captain in the Valley City Guards before the war, and when the Third Michigan was mustered, he commanded Company K. Pierce's promotions included major (October 21, 1861), lieutenant colonel (July 25, 1862) and colonel (January 1, 1863). Promotion to brigadier general (June 7, 1864) led to brigade command, and Pierce's brigade saw extensive action in the Petersburg and Appomattox Campaigns. During the final days of the war, Pierce's brigade had spectacular success at the Battle of Sailor's Creek, which earned the general a brevet promotion to major general.

Several other Pierce family members also saw wartime service. Lieutenant Silas Pierce, who began his army career in the Fourth Michigan Cavalry, served on his brother's staff during the latter days of the war. Another brother, Edwin S. Pierce, entered the service in May 1861 as captain of Company E, Third Michigan Infantry. In January 1863, at the urging of fellow officers, he was

Byron R. Pierce, a Grand Rapids dentist, went to war in June 1861 as a captain of Company K, Third Michigan Infantry. By war's end, he had survived four wounds and earned honors as a brevet major general. *Courtesy of the State Archives of Michigan.*

promoted to lieutenant colonel. Edwin saw action at Chancellorsville and Gettysburg. At the latter, he briefly assumed regimental command after his brother fell wounded. Poor health led Edwin Pierce to resign his commission in January 1864. Another family member, Major Henry C. Grout, a U.S. Army paymaster, was married to General Pierce's sister.[27]

CHANCELLORSVILLE, GETTYSBURG AND BEYOND

The Third Michigan missed the Battle of Antietam and saw only limited action at the Battle of Fredericksburg. That situation changed considerably, as the Army of the Potomac resumed campaigning in April 1863. At Chancellorsville, the Third was heavily engaged and through "stubborn fighting" suffered sixty-three casualties. Then there was Gettysburg.[28]

On June 11, 1863, the men of the Third Michigan exchanged their Austrian rifles for Enfields, filled their haversacks with three days of cooked rations and broke camp near Falmouth, Virginia. The Army of the Potomac was headed north, responding to the Rebel invasion of Pennsylvania. The oppressive June weather took a heavy toll on the Yankees. After a few days of marching, Captain Daniel S. Root of Grand Rapids recorded in his diary, "The day was terribly hot, not a breath of air. The dust almost suffocating and no water to be obtained. We marched incessantly and without mercy....The road was literally strewn with the dead and dying from the effect of the heat." Despite the marching challenges, there were a few positive moments. In Maryland, the houses displayed the Stars and Stripes, and as Captain Root recorded, "people are decidedly friendly" toward the Yankee soldiers. Among the many challenges, the Army of the Potomac also welcomed a new army commander—Fifth Corps commander Major General George Meade. Captain Root was unimpressed. "The feeling in the army is one of indifference. The men have learned to place less dependence on their generals; they know that the men and not the generals decide the battles. All they ask is to face the foe."[29]

Twenty-year-old William Prindle of Grand Rapids joined the Third Michigan Infantry in May 1861. Captured at the Battle of the Wilderness, he died in late April 1865 after enduring what was described as "barbarous treatment" while imprisoned in Florence, South Carolina. *Courtesy of Dave Broene.*

Captain Root soon got his wish. Notwithstanding cloudbursts that turned roads into quagmires, the Third Michigan arrived at Gettysburg in the mid-morning of July 2—the second day of the battle. The Third was one of the smallest regiments in Colonel Régis de Trobriand's brigade, Birney's Division, Third Corps. When Major General Dan Sickles advanced his Third Corps from the Union position on Cemetery Ridge, de Trobriand's brigade formed along the southern edge of a field of grain that soon became known simply as "The Wheatfield." The Third Michigan's right flank connected with troops in the Peach Orchard. As the battle unfolded on the late afternoon of July 2, advancing Rebels pressed the Third Corps. The Third engaged the enemy around the Rose farm, and as Lieutenant Colonel Pierce later reported, sometimes the volleys were being exchanged "at a range of not over 50 yards." As the Union position in the Peach Orchard eroded, the Third "retired in good order," according to Pierce. The regiment's forty-one casualties included a wounded Colonel Pierce.[30]

The Third saw no more fighting at Gettysburg, but on July 3, the Michiganians attended to wounded Rebels from General George Pickett's failed charge. In the days immediately following the battle, twenty-one-year-old Andrew Kilpatrick of Grand Rapids noted, "Our men are all busy burying the dead, and picking up arms. Many wandering over the field looking at the terrible sights caused by the determined strife." The Third Michigan remained at Gettysburg for several days, leaving on July 7, much to the relief of one Michiganian, who noted that "a very bad odor" began rising from the battlefield. After reaching Virginia, the Third headed north for an unanticipated mission—maintaining civil order as protestors rebelled against conscription. After arriving in New York City, which had just endured the nation's worst draft riot, the Third moved up the Hudson River to Troy, New York. Two weeks later, with peace restored, the Third rejoined the Army of Potomac in Virginia.[31]

In late 1863, 207 of the regiment's "Boys of 1861" reenlisted for the duration of the war. When campaigning in Virginia resumed on May 4, 1864, the Third Michigan soon experienced intense and bloody fighting at the Battles of the Wilderness and Spotsylvania. Losses during the month of May totaled 31 killed, 119 wounded and 29 missing. On June 9, 1864, the Third Michigan was pulled from the battle line. Those who had reenlisted for the duration were formed into four companies and attached to the Fifth Michigan Infantry Regiment. Those whose terms of service had expired headed home and were mustered out of federal service in Detroit on June 20. The Third Michigan Infantry ceased to exist. According to the official *Record of Service*, 1,432 officers and enlisted men served in the Third Michigan Infantry. Losses totaled: killed in action (110), died of wounds (65), died in prison camps (15) and died of disease (81).[32]

POSTWAR ACCOLADES

At Spotsylvania, twenty-two-year-old Benjamin Morse, who had joined the Third Michigan in May 1861, captured the flag of the Fourth Georgia

An Irish immigrant, Daniel Crotty served the entire war, first in the Third Michigan Infantry and then the Fifth Michigan Infantry. After the Battle of Chancellorsville, he was awarded the Kearny Cross, which Crotty wears proudly in this picture. After the war, he married Anne McMahon of Grand Rapids; they had nine children. *Courtesy of the State Archives of Michigan.*

Battery. Twenty-seven years later, Morse, who lived in Lowell, received the Medal of Honor for his actions at Spotsylvania. He had served the entire war, was wounded once and captured twice (White Oak and Chancellorsville).[33]

Born in Ireland, twenty-one-year-old Daniel G. Crotty settled in Grand Rapids sometime before the Civil War and enlisted in Company F, Third Michigan, on May 13, 1861. Crotty reenlisted in December 1863 and was mustered out on July 5, 1865. In 1900, he claimed his actions at the Battle of the Wilderness warranted the Medal of Honor. Retired officers concurred that Crotty "was seen carrying the flag forward into the very front of the enemy." But the Irish color sergeant never received the medal. After the war, Crotty returned to Michigan, marrying Anne McMahon at St. Andrews Church in Grand Rapids; they had nine children. In 1874, Crotty published *Four Years Campaigning in the Army of the Potomac*. Since he did

Nineteen-year-old Benjamin Morse of Grand Rapids went to war in June 1861 with the Third Michigan Infantry. Years after the war, Morse received the Medal of Honor for capturing a Rebel flag at the Battle of Spotsylvania. *Author's collection.*

not keep a journal or diary during the war, critics charged that *Campaigning* "appears to be based solely on Crotty's vague recollections rather than any hard evidence." Crotty did not use other works or diaries, and "this lack of attention to specifics," according to one critic, "combined with a flowery style of prose makes the work greatly suspect as to its veracity." Even with these shortcomings, Daniel Crotty's 207-page work contains some valuable insights into the life of a Union soldier and is worth reading.[34]

A CITY OF HORSE SOLDIERS

The duties of cavalry are as arduous, complex and diversified as it is possible for any branch of the military service to be.
—Colonel S.H. Hastings, Fifth Michigan Cavalry

During the Civil War, Grand Rapids might also have been labeled "Michigan's Horse Soldier City," since almost half of the state's cavalry regiments originated in the Valley City. As one veteran Michigan cavalry officer observed after the war, "The duties of cavalry are as arduous, complex and diversified as it is possible for any branch of the military service to be....[A good cavalryman] must pass through a long course of drill training, both mounted and dismounted; and if any one imagines that even a hard and thorough course of drill training entirely fits a trooper for active campaign service, he will find himself much mistaken."[35]

Unlike the rush to volunteer for infantry service after the Rebel attack on Fort Sumter, cavalry was a different matter. U.S. Army officials, including Commanding General Winfield Scott and Secretary of War Simon Cameron, neither asked for nor favored volunteer cavalry. Outfitting a cavalryman was an expensive proposition—an estimated $14,000 to arm, equip, mount and maintain a regiment for one year. Equally important, producing a skilled trooper took up to two years of training. In 1861, neither the U.S. government budget nor the perceived length of the war supported enlisting volunteer cavalrymen. Finally, it was believed that the heavily wooded Virginia countryside, with its numerous rivers and streams, would keep cavalry from playing a significant tactical role. Congress added another regiment to the existing five regiments of regular cavalry, but that left the army with only 6,000 troopers. This shortsighted view changed after the Yankee defeat at Bull Run in mid-July 1861 when General Irwin McDowell's army fielded a cavalry force of fewer than 500 men. The day after the battle, the U.S. government included cavalrymen in its call for 500,000 volunteers. Michigan took the lead and, by war's end, supplied more cavalrymen in proportion of population than any other Northern state.[36]

VALLEY CITY CAVALRY, PART ONE

First Michigan Cavalry

Shortly after the Battle of First Bull Run, Colonel Thornton Brodhead opened cavalry recruiting offices in Detroit and Grand Rapids. A few days later, the *Grand Rapids Weekly Enquirer* boasted that "this arm of the service seems to be quite a favorite [as men]…were rushing" to join. One Grand Rapids–based recruiting officer sought out backwoodsmen who were "not only first class riders, but also crack shots." Recruits from all across the state soon assembled at Camp Lyon, a hastily created training facility a few miles north of Detroit. During the next few weeks, regimental surgeon Dr. George K. Johnson of Grand Rapids performed perfunctory physicals. (Dr. Johnson left the First Michigan Cavalry in February 1863 but served the entire war as a U.S. medical inspector, earning a honorable discharge as a lieutenant colonel in October 1865.) On September 13, the First Michigan Volunteer Cavalry (with a smattering of Kent County men) was mustered into Federal service. Two weeks later, the First marched on foot to the Detroit train depot, where the men boarded trains for Washington, D.C. (Their horses followed later.) After reaching the nation's capital, the Michiganians bivouacked about a mile east of the U.S. Capitol—an area quickly renamed Camp Brodhead, after the regiment's commander.[37]

Arrival in the capital failed to excite some men. In late November, one trooper complained, "I do not believe that we will ever be called to make a field campaign, or take part in a battle, so we simply have to be satisfied with lying around until they send us home again." How wrong he was. The arrival of the regiment's horses was followed by months of active operations. Beginning in late February 1862, the First moved into the Shenandoah

Valley, part of a force designed to preoccupy local Rebel forces from threatening General George McClellan's Peninsula Campaign in eastern Virginia. Dealing with snow, mud and plenty of Rebels, the First Michigan saw considerable action. Despite some initial success, the First belonged to an army tormented by Rebel general Stonewall Jackson in his famed Valley Campaign. By mid-July 1862, the Michiganians were part of the newly created Army of Virginia commanded by General John Pope. The First suffered sizeable losses at the humiliating Yankee defeat at the Second Battle of Bull Run in late August, including mortally wounded Colonel Brodhead, as well as dozens of troopers taken prisoner. The First Michigan missed the bloody fights at Antietam and Fredericksburg before experiencing a major change in its mission in June 1863, when it joined three other Michigan regiments to form one of the war's fightingest units.[38]

Second and Third Michigan Cavalries

An abundance of enthusiasm to fill the ranks of the First Michigan Cavalry sparked the interest of Congressman Francis C. Kellogg, whose west Michigan district included Grand Rapids. As the First Michigan prepared to go to war, Kellogg received permission from the War Department and Governor Austin Blair to form the Second and Third Michigan Cavalries in Grand Rapids.[39]

Early arrangements for the Second Michigan proved hectic, even "very imperfect," according to the regimental historian. Buildings at Camp Anderson, previously occupied by the Third Michigan Infantry, housed the troopers as they arrived in Grand Rapids. Camp shortages led these future veterans to chuckle years later how naïve they were complaining about "a rusty fork" or slightly burned soup. As these men experienced, campaigning led to greater challenges and worse conditions.[40]

West Michigan was well represented in the Second Michigan with companies from Grand Rapids (C), Holland (D) and Lowell (F). Russell A. Alger commanded the "Grand Rapids company." A native Ohioan whose English ancestors had arrived in Massachusetts in 1627, Alger relocated in Grand Rapids in 1860. Despite having studied law, Alger did not hang out his shingle but entered the lumbering business. The year after arriving in Michigan, he also married Annette H. Henry of Grand Rapids; the couple eventually had six children. Ben Smith of Pine Plains (Allegan County) commanded the Holland men. According to regimental historian Marshal

Eighteen-year-old Thales L. Chapin of Kent County went to war with the Second Michigan Cavalry in September 1861. He served the entire conflict, mustering out in August 1865. *Author's collection.*

Twenty-eight-year-old Joseph Palmer of Wright Township (Ottawa County) enlisted in the Second Michigan Cavalry in September 1861. He ended his military career as a first lieutenant in August 1865. *Courtesy of Dave Broene.*

P. Thatcher, Smith "would sit up later and work harder for a joke than any man in the regiment." Presumably, Smith's leadership skills went beyond joke telling. According to Thatcher, Company D "gave a good account of themselves…whether the captain or his wife" commanded the Hollanders.[41]

Leaving Grand Rapids on November 14, the Second Michigan Cavalry traveled to Detroit before moving on to St. Louis, Missouri, where the Michiganians met their first regimental commander, Colonel Gordon Granger, a West Pointer who had seen action several months earlier at the Battle of Wilson's Creek, Missouri. Following Granger's short tenure with the Second Michigan, Captain (soon to be Colonel) Philip H. Sheridan succeeded him. Not long after Sheridan arrived, the Michiganians tangled with Rebels on July 1, 1862, near Boonville, Mississippi. Captain Alger, one of the heroes of this spirited skirmish, led a handpicked force of about one hundred men on a surprise mission. According to Sheridan, Alger "handsomely conducted" his role in driving the much larger enemy force from the field. In the process, Alger earned a promotion to major and, according to one hometown historian, shined in "one of the most notable of the minor achievements of the war." After Sheridan moved on to higher command and greater fame, the Second saw action at Perryville, Chickamauga, the Atlanta Campaign, Franklin and numerous lesser-known engagements, compiling "a record of which the State, as well as Grand Rapids, [was] justly proud."[42]

Six weeks after the Second Cavalry left the state, the Third Michigan Cavalry mustered into Federal service in Grand Rapids. The unit's companies came from towns all across Michigan, with little Kent County representation, except for the unit's first colonel, Congressman Kellogg. However, lacking any military experience (and presumably disinterested in relinquishing his political job), Kellogg resigned his commission on March 7, 1862. However, Grand Rapids was well represented among the regiment's quartermasters—William W. Cantine, Chauncy C. Douglass, Henry Jewett and Mortimer L. Hopkins. Of the four men, Cantine remained with the Third until October 1865, leaving service as a brevet major.[43]

Like the Second, the Third Michigan saw service in the war's western theater. During the hectic year of 1863, the Third marched "more than 10,000 miles, exclusive of marches in separate companies and detachments." During the last year of the war, the Third was garrisoned at Brownsville Station, Arkansas, where it "erected a complete set of winter quarters and stables, so neatly and tastefully arranged as to present the appearance of an important town." The efforts of the Third attracted so much attention that there were suggestions about changing the town's name to "Michigan City."[44]

VALLEY CITY CAVALRY, PART TWO

Sixth Michigan Cavalry

More than a year into the war, the Army of the Potomac cavalry needed strengthening, and Congressman Kellogg received the authority to form the Sixth and Seventh Regiments. As plans for these two regiments evolved, the Fifth Michigan Cavalry was being organized in Detroit. General recruiting enthusiasm led the Fifth to send an overflow of several hundred recruits to Grand Rapids. Among those early recruits was an exceptional wartime observer.[45]

In June 1862, twenty-two-year-old James H. Kidd of Ionia had just finished his sophomore year at the University of Michigan. A year earlier, Kidd had organized the Tappan Guard, a home guard of students named after university president Henry Tappan. Kidd familiarized himself with *Hardee's Tactics* and trained his company with plans on joining the Twenty-First Michigan Infantry. Kidd's enthusiasm earned him an offer for an officer's commission with the Twenty-First, but he had cavalry on his mind.

Left: After finishing his sophomore year at the University of Michigan, twenty-two-year-old James Kidd of Ionia raised a company of men, received an officer's commission and joined the Sixth Michigan Cavalry. His postwar recollections are among the best composed by any Michiganian. *Courtesy of Bentley Historical Library, University of Michigan.*

His father's respected position in the Grand Rapids business community aided Kidd's conversion to cavalry. The elder Kidd was "one of the most energetic and honorable businessmen in the Grand River valley" and enjoyed political connections with Congressman Kellogg and various prominent Valley City men like Wilder D. Foster, whom Kidd described as a "big friend" with "a big heart and an open hand." These connections undoubtedly helped Kidd receive a "conditional" officer's appointment. The condition? He had to enlist seventy-eight men in fifteen days. (Kidd was granted four additional days when the two weeks expired.) A skilled politician, Kellogg made the same "conditional" deal with three others. Kidd conceded finding enlistees "was no easy task," since the area had been "very thoroughly canvassed." However, he surpassed his rivals and arrived in Grand Rapids in mid-September where he became captain of Company E, Sixth Michigan Cavalry.

Right: Irish native George Gray settled in Grand Rapids in 1855. A lawyer noted for his "urbanity," Gray served as city attorney. He commanded the Sixth Michigan Cavalry from its formation in October 1862 until his honorable discharge in May 1864. *From Kidd, Personal Recollections.*

Acting on a suggestion from Colonel Joseph Copeland, the newly designated commander of the Fifth Michigan Cavalry, Governor Blair appointed George Gray, a native of Ireland who arrived in Grand Rapids in 1855, as lieutenant colonel of the Sixth. A successful and accomplished lawyer, "who had no equal before a jury," the thirty-nine-year-old Gray earned praise for the "sterling integrity of his character [and] the urbanity of his disposition." Although a good "after dinner speaker," Gray lacked any previous military experience and "had an irascible temper at times." Captain Kidd labeled Gray "something of a martinet." Gray's love of the bottle, which left him "erratic and undependable," coupled with his dislike of the press, contributed to his resignation in early 1864. But those problems lay in the future. As the unit was being formed in Grand Rapids, the regiment's officers circulated a petition that led the governor to promote Gray to colonel in mid-October.[46]

The Sixth's most prominent field officer needed little introduction, especially after the publicity following the Boonville, Mississippi skirmish. Twenty-six-year-old Lieutenant Colonel Russell A. Alger was "tall, erect, handsome," a distinct contrast with Gray, who was balding and ruddy-faced. Meticulous in his appearance, Alger offered the "body language of a man used to command, with no need to swagger." An expert horseman who took over the unit's training, the "always cool and self poised" Alger possessed

A native New Yorker, twenty-seven-year-old Elijah D. Waters moved to Grand Rapids in 1857. He worked at his brother's meatpacking business before joining the Sixth Michigan Cavalry as a major in October 1862. When the Sixth traveled to Washington, D.C., the regiment faced innumerable delays. Claiming "they ran the road," unsympathetic officials rejected the major's request to stop the train so the men and horses could eat. An annoyed Waters conceded that they might run "the road," but he was running "that train." Waters ordered the train to a siding to accomplish the much-needed feeding. A postwar observer noted, "His men lustily cheered him for his act of kindness." Poor health forced Waters to resign his commission in May 1863. *From Baxter,* History of the City of Grand Rapids, Michigan.

a voice so clear that the entire regiment—all 1,200 men when formed in a single rank—"distinctly" heard his commands. According to Kidd, Alger "had few equals and no superiors" as a battalion commander. However, Alger possessed "impulsive and impetuous" tendencies and, as an inspiring politician, his "political skills warred with his responsibilities as an officer." (To be fair, Kidd offered this postwar judgment after Alger had held several key political positions—both elected and appointed.)[47]

Other field officers from Grand Rapids included Majors Thaddeus Foote and Elijah D. Waters. A lawyer, Foote served with the Sixth for a year before moving on to command the Tenth Michigan Cavalry. Waters saw little field service, leaving the army in May 1863. Two other line officers with prior experience included Captain Peter A. Weber and Lieutenant Don G. Lovell. Both had gone to war as corporals with the Third Michigan Infantry. Lovell suffered a wound during the Peninsula Campaign, while Weber served in the Second Michigan Cavalry as a junior officer before transferring to the Sixth. Weber was "fitted by nature and acquirements for much higher rank than any he held." He also possessed a "penetrating and musical quality that made it easy to hear him when he was making no apparent effort to be heard." In his postwar memories, Captain Kidd remembered his first meeting with Weber, a former Grand Rapids store clerk, on a rainy day:

> *He looked younger than his years, was not large, but had a well-knit, compact frame of medium height. He was alert in look and movement, his face was ruddy with health, his eyes bright and piercing, his head*

crowned with a thick growth of brown hair cut rather short. He wore a forage cap, a gum coat over his uniform, top boots, and appeared every inch a soldier.

Weber commanded Company B. As for Lovell, Kidd recalled him as "one of the bravest of the brave." Captain Henry E. Thompson commanded Company A, a troop that had been organized for three months and "attracted a good deal of attention [for being] well drilled and disciplined [and] fully uniformed." Its junior officers included Lieutenants Manning D. Birge, Stephen H. Ballard and Joel S. Sheldon (all of Grand Rapids). (Thompson and Birge rose to field command, while Ballard survived six months in a Rebel prison.)[48]

Another Grand Rapids officer who rose to distinction was assistant surgeon David C. Spaulding. Kidd recalled Dr. Spaulding's unique cure for one trooper who had feigned sickness in hopes of earning a disability discharge. After only a week of treatment, the man promised to do his job as long as he

Peter A. Weber began his military career with the Second Michigan Cavalry before joining the Sixth Michigan Cavalry. Among the city's most popular officers, Weber was killed leading a senseless charge at Falling Waters, Maryland, on July 14, 1863. *From Kidd,* Personal Recollections.

never had to return to the hospital where they "will kill me." When asked about his amazing cure, Spaulding explained the patient "was purged, cupped, blistered, given emetics, until life really became a burden and he ran away from the 'treatment.'" Dr. Spaulding left the Sixth in mid-1863 to become the chief surgeon for the Tenth Michigan Cavalry. The Reverend Stephen S.N. Greeley served as the Sixth's regimental chaplain throughout the war. Arriving in Grand Rapids in 1857, Greeley ministered at the First Congregational Church, one of the city's oldest congregations. Kidd characterized Greeley as "a unique character…a powerful pulpit orator, a kind-hearted, simple-minded gentleman of the old school." Quartermaster Lieutenant Charles H. Patten, also from Grand Rapids, served as an "honest, energetic and capable" quartermaster. Patten earned the highest possible praise since "his wagon trains never failed to reach the front…when it was possible to get them there."[49]

After three months of training in Grand Rapids, the recruits of the Sixth Michigan Cavalry "looked something like cavalrymen…as they stood clad in their jackboots, reinforced pantaloons and natty jackets, their caps and slouch caps at a rakish style." According to historian Edward Longacre, the troopers expressed "a patina of professionalism." The cavaliers were armed with rapid-firing, breech-loading carbines "that proved decisive on more than one field of battle." The regiment also grouped its horses by color. According to Kidd, "it was a grand sight" when the 1,200 horses were lined up or paraded. However, this arrangement only lasted a few months.[50]

The Sixth Michigan Cavalry mustered into service on October 13, 1862 (following its sister regiment, the Fifth, by six weeks). Two months later, on a bright moonlit December evening, the Sixth headed to the Grand Rapids train depot. After several days of travel, during which the Michiganians received many "hearty and affectionate greetings" along the way, the Sixth arrived in the nation's capital and camped at Camp Copeland atop Meridian Hill, north of the White House.[51]

Seventh Michigan Cavalry

While the Sixth headed to war, the Seventh Michigan Cavalry remained in Grand Rapids, struggling to get organized. Detroiter William Mann, formerly a major in the First Michigan Cavalry, arrived in the Valley City expecting to command the Sixth Michigan Cavalry. Instead, influential Grand Rapids residents pressed Governor Blair to appoint local resident George Gray colonel of the Sixth. Blair offered Mann command of the Seventh. Frustrated and feeling misled, Mann recalled his "first impulse" was to retire from the service. However, he decided that his "ambition, tastes, nervous energy or patriotism" would not allow him to quit and accepted the colonelcy of the Seventh.[52]

Mann faced numerous early obstacles, especially lagging enlistment. Recruiting bounties had lost their appeal, and the draft seemed no more than a rumor. The war had turned bloody and—combined with thirteen dollars a month and lousy rations—it did not seem worth the risk. However, Mann and his second in command, Lieutenant Colonel Allyn C. Litchfield (Blendon, Ottawa County), lobbied hard, and the regiment's ranks slowly filled.[53]

Left: Twenty-year-old Henry M. Nevins of Grand Rapids joined the Seventh Michigan Cavalry as a second lieutenant on January 1, 1863. *Courtesy of the State Archives of Michigan.*

Right: James Rathbun of Caledonia entered the Sixth Michigan Cavalry as a wagoner in September 1862. He survived the war, mustering out in June 1865. *Courtesy of Dave Broene.*

Learning soldiering was demanding, especially when drill instructors greeted mistakes, as one Seventh veteran recalled, with "a volley of blood-curdling oaths," while another expressed his outrage by hurtling small rocks at offenders. Camp conditions also proved challenging. The regimental historian recalled the rough-board, one-story-high barracks "were like sieves, through which the keen, cold air circulated freely. It was too cold to sit down, and meals were therefore eaten standing, with every muscle in the body undergoing exercise." At night, the men huddled around the stoves, "giving no heed to the demand for sleep, in the endeavor to keep warm and 'wishing for the war to cease.'" Despite those inconveniences, the Seventh boasted about its horses, a tribute to First Lieutenant and Quartermaster Farnham Lyon of Grand Rapids.[54]

In early 1863, with only ten of the necessary twelve squadrons filled, the Seventh Michigan Cavalry was sworn into Federal service and, a month later, headed to Washington, D.C. The men dejectedly remembered the low-key sendoff. "No ladies appeared upon the scene" to present the men with housewives, havelocks or even a farewell lunch. Major Henry W. Granger of Grand Rapids, formerly of the First New York Cavalry, remained behind with a small command to care for the barracks and continue recruiting Companies L and M. When 1e Seventh arrived in the nation's capital, it camped near the Sixth.[55]

Winter in Washington proved challenging for the Michigan cavalrymen. The mud and cold posed the biggest obstacle. Captain Kidd discovered "wide streets of mud," while another Michigan trooper noted their horses were "knee-deep in the cold ooze [and] without shelter." The miserable conditions contributed to illnesses—pneumonia, rheumatism, typhoid fever and measles, even smallpox—and the sick lists grew longer with each passing week. One member of the Seventh recalled nothing was "more thoroughly miserable" than those first weeks.[56]

VALLEY CITY CAVALRY, PART THREE

Michigan Cavalry Brigade and the Battle of Gettysburg

After weeks of drilling, the Fifth, Sixth and Seventh Michigan moved out of the capital into the countryside. Brigaded together under the command of Brigadier General Joseph Copeland of Pontiac, Michigan, the "Michigan Cavalry Brigade" (as it was soon known) concentrated its energies on capturing the noted Rebel guerilla John Mosby. Bagging the elusive "Gray Ghost" proved too challenging for the inexperienced Michigan cavaliers, but that did not mean the expeditions lacked satisfying moments. On several patrols, the Sixth Michigan Cavalry detained deserters. "We have captured men enough to form a company," a correspondent boasted. During these expeditions, the cavaliers also forced "quite a number" of disloyal sympathizers to take the oath of allegiance, which earned them "the contempt and hatred" of local secessionists. Understandably, officers proved essential in these undertakings, and the Sixth Michigan boasted among the best. "Our officers are not the men to be tampered with, as more than one hoary-headed traitor can testify," an observer recorded. He continued, "They perform their duties fearlessly....Capt. [Harvey H.] Vinton [Vergennes, Kent County] is the rock

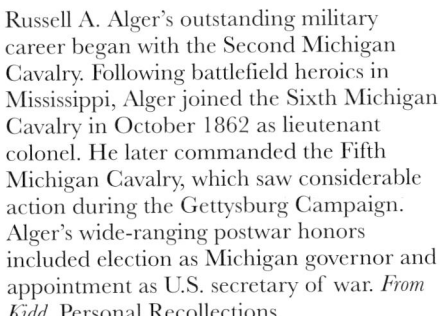

Russell A. Alger's outstanding military career began with the Second Michigan Cavalry. Following battlefield heroics in Mississippi, Alger joined the Sixth Michigan Cavalry in October 1862 as lieutenant colonel. He later commanded the Fifth Michigan Cavalry, which saw considerable action during the Gettysburg Campaign. Alger's wide-ranging postwar honors included election as Michigan governor and appointment as U.S. secretary of war. *From Kidd,* Personal Recollections.

on which we all lean. He has won the hearts of all his men by his kind and gentlemanly deportment." On another occasion, searching for horses and contraband, the cavaliers found a fine gray mare concealed by her owners *inside* their house. The Yankees took the horse despite protests by the lady of the house, whose "mildest wish" was that the first Yankee who mounted the horse would break his neck. The Michigan Cavalry Brigade missed the Chancellorsville Campaign in early May, as well as the war's biggest cavalry battle (Brandy Station, Virginia, June 9). However, the Michiganians soon learned what hard fighting meant as the Gettysburg Campaign unfolded.[57]

On June 20, the War Department placed the Michigan Cavalry Brigade under the jurisdiction of the Army of the Potomac. Several days later, the Michigan troopers forded the mile-wide Potomac on a cloudy night, with the raging waters "nearly at the top of saddles," as one soldier remembered. Although the Michiganians crossed safely, another recorded that "our boots filled with water and our pants, thoroughly soaked to our knees, added none to our comfort." The brigade's misery was heightened when the supply train was delayed. "Wet, weary and chilled to the marrow," the Michiganians bivouacked for the night at Pooleville, Maryland. Conditions brightened the next day in Frederick when local citizens enthusiastically greeted the cavaliers with cheers and smiles. The presence of ample U.S. flags led one Michigan trooper to observe, "This is a beautiful place."[58]

On Sunday, June 28, the Fifth and Sixth Michigan arrived at Gettysburg, Pennsylvania, and local citizens eagerly turned out "to see so many of our own men," as one local resident recalled. It proved a refreshing contrast to the "dirty mean-looking rebels" who had passed through town a few days earlier. Residents showed their appreciation by offering "pails of water, or apple butter [and] immense platters of bread." Women and girls also expressed their gratitude, and Captain Kidd recalled that "every man had a bunch of flowers in his hand, or a wreath around his neck." They even decorated the horses. Lieutenant Colonel Alger later observed, "Such a demonstration of joy…it has never been my privilege to witness either before or since."[59]

General Copeland dispatched companies to cover the many roads radiating from the soon-to-be-famous town. Confirming that the Rebel army was less than a day's march to the west and north, he sent word of his discovery to Union forces at Frederick, Maryland. Copeland followed orders and left Gettysburg before daylight, despite pleas from residents who begged the troopers to stay. South of Gettysburg, a courier met the Michiganians with a communiqué that changed the brigade's future. The Michigan Cavalry Brigade, with the addition of the First Michigan Cavalry, had been transferred to the Army of the Potomac, Copeland relieved of command and First Lieutenant George Armstrong Custer appointed the new brigadier. Ironically, Custer (West Point, class of 1860) had sought the command of either the Fifth or the Seventh Michigan Cavalries, but political differences prevented that from becoming a reality. (Governor Austin Blair was Republican, and Custer came from a family of Democrats.) In May 1863, Custer served on the staff of Alfred Pleasanton, the new commander of the Army of the Potomac Cavalry Corps. Pleasanton received permission to advance "officers with the proper dash to command cavalry," and no one who knew Custer accused him of lacking flair. In an army where seniority was sacred, Custer and two other junior officers (Hugh Judson Kilpatrick and Elon Farnsworth) enjoyed the rare phenomena of skipping several grades to be appointed brigadier general. Custer assumed command of the Michigan Cavalry Brigade dressed in what was described as "more costume than uniform," with one officer comparing the young brigadier to "a circus rider gone mad."[60]

On June 30, the Michigan Cavalry Brigade tangled with Rebel cavalry east of Gettysburg as General J.E.B. Stuart's troopers struggled to join the Army of Northern Virginia after an unanticipated six-day absence. The fight began when Colonel Gray's Sixth Michigan encountered Wade Hampton's Southern brigade. Badly outnumbered, Gray pulled back, but he ordered Major Peter A. Weber to command a two-company rear guard. As Kidd recorded later, the twenty-two-year-old Weber performed "gallantly,"

Twenty-nine-year-old Charles E. Storrs (Blendon, Ottawa County) entered the Sixth Michigan Cavalry as a second lieutenant in late 1862. Wounded once in the war, he mustered out as a major in October 1865. *From Kidd,* Personal Recollections.

repulsing three enemy charges. Finally driven from the field, Weber and his men rejoined the regiment hours later. Fighting elsewhere on the battlefield, the Fifth Michigan—led by recently promoted Colonel Alger and assisted by Captain Thompson and his Grand Rapids company from the Sixth Michigan—held its own against superior numbers. Fighting ended with darkness, and the Rebels withdrew from the battlefield. The Michiganians and their new commander had performed admirably in their first fight together.[61]

On July 2, as fighting raged around Gettysburg, the Michigan troopers once again clashed with Southern cavalry north of Gettysburg, near Hunterstown. A detachment from the Sixth Michigan, led by Lieutenant Charles E. Storrs (Blendon, Ottawa County), surprised elements of General Wade Hampton's Rebel brigade. Early in the fighting, James C. Parsons, a twenty-five-year-old from Grand Rapids, found himself engaged in a "personal" firefight with Hampton at a distance of about 125 yards. When his weapon fouled, Parsons raised his hand, seeking time to clear the bore. Hampton nodded his approval and waited patiently. When the contest resumed, the South Carolinian came out the winner, wounding Parsons and forcing him to flee. Parsons was out of the fight, but not Lieutenant Storrs, who closed on Hampton, striking the brigadier with his saber. Miraculously, the general avoided serious injury and took after his assailant. A faulty percussion cap in Hampton's pistol and a speedy horse saved Storrs from injury or capture. After a short delay, fighting resumed as Custer deployed his brigade. Once again, Captain Thompson's men saw action. However, the ill-conceived plan went poorly, and enemy—as well as friendly—fire, coupled with the darkness, thwarted the Yankee effort. Casualties included a severely wounded Thompson, Lieutenant Stephen H. Ballard (his second-in-command, also from Grand Rapids) and two dozen Company A troopers. Ballard survived, but he was captured and spent two years in a Rebel prison. At Hanover and Hunterstown, the Michigan Cavalry Brigade, motivated by its youthful brigadier, fought a tested enemy to a standstill, further delaying Stuart's quest to rejoin Lee's army.[62]

On the morning of July 3, as the Rebels prepared to attack Cemetery Ridge, Stuart and two brigades of veteran cavalry moved around the Union right flank with orders to disrupt the rear of the Union center. If Lee's plan of pressing the Union center from both the front ("Pickett's Charge") and rear succeeded, the enemy line would be broken and the Yankees routed. During the early morning hours, the Michigan Cavalry Brigade prepared to move to the distant Union left flank south of Big Round Top. Protecting the Union right flank, General David M. Gregg feared his understrength division of cavalry outnumbered and commandeered the Michigan brigade. As Gregg deployed the Fifth and Sixth Michigan across fields north of the Hanover Road, the Yankees and Rebels exchanged gunfire. By early afternoon, neither side had gained an advantage. In the meantime, the balance of the Michigan Cavalry Brigade (First and Seventh Michigan) arrived on the field.[63]

In the first phase of an expanding struggle, Colonel Alger, Fifth Michigan commander, sent two fifty-man detachments under the command of Major Weber to act as pickets. From his forward vantage point, Weber sent back reports that General Custer later acknowledged kept him "well informed" of the enemy's movements. Elsewhere, Alger positioned his men behind a rail fence in the area of the Rummel farm and kept the Rebels busy. As "a stubborn and spirited contest" evolved, the Fifth started taking casualties, including the death of Major Noah H. Ferry, a popular officer from Grand Haven.

As the Fifth ran out of ammunition and retreated, Stuart sent his veteran First Virginia Cavalry across the Rummel farm field. Gregg countered with the Seventh Michigan. As Colonel Mann's regiment nervously prepared for its first saber attack, Custer rode up and led the men into action. As the distance of about a mile between the two forces closed, the Seventh picked up steam, urged on by Custer yelling, "Come on, you Wolverines!" The attack enjoyed some limited success until the inexperienced Michiganians encountered stubborn rail fences that created much confusion and broke up their charge. Some Yankees dismounted and struggled to remove the fences. Among those leading this effort was Adjutant George G. Briggs and Captain Heman N. Moore of Grand Rapids. Briggs's horse went down wounded. In the confusion, he grappled with several Rebels, but returned to the Union lines safely. A temporary passageway between the fences allowed some Michigan troopers to resume the charge until they encountered

Raised in Battle Creek, George G. Briggs entered the Seventh Michigan Cavalry as a first lieutenant in October 1862. After mustering out in late 1865 as the regiment's colonel, Briggs moved to Grand Rapids, married Julia R. Peirce (daughter of one of the city's earliest settlers) and became a successful businessman. During the late 1880s, Brigg served as chairman of the state commission that erected Michigan monuments on the Gettysburg battlefield. *From Kidd,* Personal Recollections.

another fence. This time, Captain Moore, whose company had lost many horses, confronted a saber-swinging Rebel. Moore avoided a direct blow, but received "the point on the back of his head" just as his horse fell wounded. Moore was taken prisoner, but in the ensuing excitement made his escape to fight another day.

Following a brief lull on the battlefield, both sides groomed themselves for the day's final act. As Stuart prepared a larger force (two regiments and one legion) to sweep the field, Gregg ordered the First Michigan forward. With Custer in the lead, the Michigan veterans drew their sabers and headed across the field. Amid a storm of cannon fire from gunners on both sides, a Yankee observer watched the Rebel cavalrymen emerge at their end of the field: "In superb form, with sabers glistening, they advanced….It was an inspiring and imposing spectacle, that brought a murmur of admiration from the [Yankee] spectators." When the two forces met, a Yankee compared the sound to "the falling of timber." Colonel Alger characterized it as the war's "most gallant charge." For several minutes, the struggle continued, with "neither side giving or asking quarter." Custer's horse went down, but the general mounted another and stayed in the fight. Other Union elements soon waded into the fight from the flanks, including unengaged elements of the Michigan Cavalry Brigade. "Slowly, stubbornly, grudgingly," according to one contemporary observer, the Rebels gave ground.

The Michigan Cavalry Brigade paid a steep price for besting North America's best cavalrymen. The First and Fifth lost about fifty men; the Sixth, fewer than a dozen; and the Seventh about one hundred—25 percent of the regiment's strength. One monumental loss was Major Ferry. After burying Ferry on the battlefield, Alger agonized, "Every moment brings a sad gloom over all our hearts for the noble Ferry."[64]

After moving to the Union right, where they spent the night, the exhausted and bloodied Michigan brigade was up early on July 4 and headed south under orders to pursue the retreating Rebel army. On the first night of the ten-day chase, the Fifth Michigan attacked a southward-bound Rebel wagon train in what Colonel Alger later described as "the hottest ordeal" of his soldiering life. In the midnight darkness, Alger's men tangled with retreating Rebels on a mountainside in the pouring rain. The Michiganians destroyed at least one hundred wagons and took 1,400 prisoners. A few days later, Alger suffered a serious leg wound that required several months of rehabilitation.[65]

The frantic and intense chase culminated on July 14 as the final elements of the Rebel army slipped back across the Potomac River. As the Sixth Michigan arrived at Falling Waters, Maryland, that morning, division commander General Kilpatrick impulsively ordered an immediate attack rather than waiting for the arrival of his main body of troops. Recognizing the formidable Rebel defenses that protected the pontoon bridges across the river, Custer ordered the Sixth Michigan to dismount and proceed cautiously. Kilpatrick demanded the Michiganians remount and make a frontal saber attack. A reluctant Custer placed one hundred troopers under the command of Captain Weber, who earlier confessed his desire to lead just such an attack. Weber's command breached the first line of defenses before the surprised Rebels recovered. In five minutes the fight was over. One Rebel later wrote, Yankee "horses without riders [were] running in every direction." In the doomed charge Grand Rapids paid a heavy price, as

Twenty-five-year-old Charles E. Bolza of Grand Rapids joined the Sixth Michigan Cavalry in October 1862. He was killed in a doomed charge chasing Robert E. Lee's Rebel army back into Virginia after the Battle of Gettysburg. *Courtesy of Grand Rapids Public Library.*

both Weber and Lieutenant Charles E. Bolza, his second in command, were killed, along with thirty other troopers wounded or taken prisoner. Later in the day, thirty-nine-year-old Major Henry W. Granger, who had once served as a Grand Rapids constable, led Seventh Michigan troopers in a successful dismounted attack on the enemy position. When the fighting ended, Kilpatrick's force had captured about five hundred prisoners and two flags. But as historian Longacre concludes, the sacrifice of Weber, Bolza and others "was a frustrating and tragic note on which to close a campaign that had witnessed some of the finest combat performances ever turned in by the cavalry of the Army of the Potomac." Despite being exhausted and bloodied after three weeks of intense campaigning, the Michigan Cavalry Brigade felt good about itself, with one trooper boasting, "Our cavalry is doing mighty things....We are now practicing war—not theorizing it."[66]

The Fighting Drags On

The rigors of constant campaigning continued after Gettysburg, and Grand Rapids area officers, especially in the Sixth Michigan Cavalry, saw plenty of action. Lieutenant George Briggs, who settled in Grand Rapids after the war, claimed, "The world has never seen such Cavalry fighting as we have done, which is the testimony of the best Cavalry officers in the service." At Buckland Mills, Virginia, a recovered Colonel Alger led a dramatic cavalry charge that extricated the Michigan Cavalry Brigade from a precarious situation. Following one charge, twenty-one-year-old Captain Daniel Powers boasted, "With drawn saber[s] flashing in the sun...we couldn't see the 'Rebs' for the dust they made" as they ran away. Another skirmish left Captain Charles E. Storrs wounded. But he returned to the Sixth and served until October 1865.[67]

In a lengthy October letter to the *Grand Rapids Daily Eagle*, one trooper assessed the Valley City's leadership in the Sixth Michigan Cavalry. The men welcomed back Lieutenant Colonel Thompson, who had recovered from his Gettysburg wound. Thompson "embodied the elements of the true soldier," and the troopers had faith in "his skill, ability and cool judgment to manage and control the affairs entrusted to him." The writer praised the newly promoted Major Kidd: "A young man of fine military talents, a true soldier, and a gentleman in the positive sense of the term." Kidd never asked his men "to go where he would not." Captain Birge, a "generous noble and brave man, a true soldier and philanthropist and a genuine patriot,"

Don G. Lovell of Grand Rapids went to war in June 1861 as a corporal in the Third Michigan Infantry. After recovering from a wound received at the Battle of Fair Oaks, he joined the Sixth Michigan Cavalry as a second lieutenant. Wounded again at Trevilian Station, Lovell was characterized as "one of the bravest of the brave." He left the army in late 1865 as a brevet major. *From Kidd, Personal Recollections.*

commanded Company A. The writer emphatically admired Lieutenant Don G. Lovell, who had gone to war in June 1861 as a corporal in the Third Michigan Infantry. Transferring to the Sixth Cavalry when the regiment was mustered, Lovell "was in his element when fighting the 'Johnnies.'" As a "true and brave soldier," Lovell "has been firm, meritorious and substantial, and as a soldier boy from Grand Rapids, is one of whom the citizens may not be ashamed." Lovell served with the Sixth until November 1865. First Lieutenant Charles H. Patten also earned recognition as a quartermaster who excelled in "actively [employing the] powers of locomotion."[68]

The winter of 1863–64 brought a welcome respite from campaigning. At the same time, the remainder of the brigade received Spencer seven-shot repeating carbines. New Michigan recruits restored the brigade to more than two thousand men—although 40 percent were "unseasoned, inexperienced, and entirely unreliable in a crisis." Colonel Gray, who had been away from the Sixth during much of the fall and winter for disability, tried unsuccessfully to rejoin the unit. Unfairly charged by critics as a "malingerer," Gray resigned in the spring of 1864. Major Kidd assumed command of the Fifth, while Major Granger, who had started his career as a lieutenant in the First New York Cavalry, assumed command of the Seventh after Colonel William Mann's resignation.[69]

As spring campaigning began in early May 1864, the Michigan Cavalry Brigade skirmished with J.E.B. Stuart's cavalry at Todd's Tavern, part of the bloody Wilderness Campaign. During the course of fighting, the Fifth Michigan played an important role, leading Kidd to credit Alger's timely arrival that aided the beleaguered Sixth Michigan and turned "a threatened reverse into a magnificent victory." A few days later, the Army of the Potomac Cavalry Corps, now led by Philip Sheridan, challenged Stuart's cavaliers at Yellow Tavern. After his men spent much of the day exchanging fire with the enemy, Sheridan ordered a mounted charge, with the Michigan Cavalry Brigade in the lead. The Fifth and Sixth provided covering fire as the First Michigan attacked over a field filled with obstacles (fences and a narrow bridge). After the First captured several Rebel cannons, Custer ordered Major Granger to advance the Seventh to carry on the offense. Suddenly—and inexplicably—the regiment's second in command turned and headed to the rear, followed by most of his men. The few men who stayed with Granger were taken prisoner, but the major was killed. Custer eulogized, "I never saw a man go more gallantly about the work before him than he did. He was a splendid man; too bad, too bad."[70]

During the first week of June 1864, Sheridan's cavalry set out on an elaborate raid designed both to disrupt a major Rebel supply line from the Shenandoah Valley and allow the Army of the Potomac to steal a march on Lee's army. As a day of fighting unfolded near Trevilian Station, northwest of Richmond, Major Kidd led the Sixth Michigan riding a powerful black charger that a fellow officer asked him to break. As the Yankees engaged the Rebels, Kidd's horse bolted, raced beyond his men and landed the major into the equally surprised hands of the enemy. Surrounded and clearly outnumbered, Kidd surrendered. However, as the captors escorted him to the rear, Major Birge ordered his battalion forward. In the confusion, Kidd gained his freedom, avoiding a Rebel prison. An appreciative Kidd reflected years later that "no man on this earth" had earned his greater indebtedness than Manning Birge. After a long day of fighting, Custer's brigade suffered four hundred casualties, including Captain Don G. Lovell, who survived his wound and returned to active duty until November 1865.[71]

During the late summer, the Michigan Cavalry Brigade transferred to the Shenandoah Valley as part of Sheridan's Army of the Shenandoah. At the September 19 Battle of Winchester, Custer's brigade participated in a dramatic charge that swept the field. Custer reported many "instances of personal daring and gallantry." Changes in Sheridan's army moved Custer to division command and promoted Colonel James Kidd to brigade command, "an unsought and an unwelcome responsibility," he later recorded. One change that generated controversy involved the resignation of Colonel Russell Alger for family health reasons. Alger's final days in the army led to accusations of absence without leave—a charge that dogged him during his postwar career.[72]

The Michigan Cavalry Brigade saw limited action during the October 19 Battle of Cedar Creek, which ended organized Rebel resistance in the

Left: Twenty-three-year-old Manning D. Birge of Grand Rapids mustered into Company A, Sixth Michigan Cavalry, as first lieutenant in late 1862. At Trevilian Station in June 1864, Birge led an impromptu charge that allowed a much-appreciative Colonel James Kidd to escape his Rebel captors. Birge mustered out at the end of the war as a major. *From Kidd, Personal Recollections.*

Right: Henry L. Wise of Caledonia entered the Sixth Michigan Cavalry as a captain of Company H in October 1862. In August 1863, the forty-five-year-old Wise transferred to the Eleventh Michigan Cavalry as a major. He survived the war, mustering out at the same rank. *Courtesy of the State Archives of Michigan.*

Valley. During the final weeks of 1864, the Michiganians actively carried out General Grant's directive to destroy any and all provisions that might aid the Rebels. According to historian Longacre, the Michiganians considered what Colonel Kidd called "a disagreeable business" both cowardly and inhuman. On one occasion, as flames from a town's flour mill engulfed nearby houses, Kidd ordered his men to help control the fire. Their efforts proved successful, but as he wrote years later, "What I saw there is burned into my memory." He explained:

> *Women and children in their arms, stood in the street and gazed frantically upon the threatened ruin of their homes, while tears rained down their cheeks. The anguish pictured in their faces would have melted any heart not seared by the horrors and "necessities" of war. It was too much for me, and at the first moment that duty would permit, I hurried away from the scene.*

General Merritt did not see these things, nor did General Sheridan, much less General Grant.[73]

Excesses continued on both sides until the winter's cold ended active campaigning.[74]

After surviving a severe winter, the Michigan Cavalry Brigade joined the Army of the Potomac at Petersburg in late March 1865. The brigade mustered about one thousand men, with Lieutenant Colonel Harvey H. Vinton (Vergennes, Kent County) commanding the Sixth. Chaplain Greeley recorded his thoughts about the trip from the Valley to Petersburg. The march proved exhausting, especially "the pain, the mud and the raging foam rivers that we have waded through." Horses who died "by the hundreds" were replaced by appropriating "a great number of fine horses from the country." The damage inflicted on the Confederacy by destroying public works, railroads, telegraphs, canals, boats and tons of provisions "cannot be estimated," as Northern armies laid to waste to "glorious old Virginia."[75]

At Petersburg, the Michigan Cavalry Brigade was actively engaged at Five Forks, the battle that forced the Rebel army to abandon Richmond. The Michigan troopers led the Yankee pursuit of Lee's fleeing army. After traveling eighty miles in five days and experiencing "the most grueling sustained march" since Gettysburg, the Michigan Cavalry Brigade arrived at a small village called Appomattox Station ahead of Lee's army. During the early morning hours of April 9, the outnumbered troopers stubbornly held their ground despite pressure from Lee's graycoats. Fighting ended abruptly when columns of blue infantry filed in behind the Yankee cavaliers. Lieutenant Colonel Briggs, commanding the Seventh Michigan, received a group of Rebel riders under a white flag and bearing Lee's note proposing a ceasefire. As Briggs escorted the truce party to General Custer, news spread and soon "cheer upon cheer went up." The war had ended—at least in Virginia.[76]

Valley City Cavalry, Part Four

Tenth Michigan Cavalry

The Tenth Michigan Cavalry, one of the state's last units sent to crush the rebellion, was organized in Grand Rapids. Colonel Thaddeus Foote of

Grand Rapids, formerly a major in the Sixth Michigan Cavalry, commanded the regiment, while Israel Canton Smith, also from Grand Rapids, served as major. Elsewhere in the unit, Captains Benjamin K. Weatherwax (Georgetown) and Elliott F. Covell (Grand Rapids) commanded Companies C and L, respectively. Grand Rapids junior officers who served throughout the war included Robert G. Barr, Frederick N. Field, Henry L. Covell, Oliver N. Taylor, Don A. Dodge and B. Franklin Sherman. After several months of campaigning, a local correspondent boasted, "If any rebels want a fight, they will surely have a chance if they fall in with" the officers of the Tenth Michigan Cavalry.[77]

Mustered into Federal service on November 18, 1863, the Tenth left the state on December 1 for Kentucky. The winter took a toll on the new regiment, causing much sickness. Marching to Knoxville in February 1864, the Tenth experienced rain, snow, sleet and ice, which left the journey, according to one participant, "very uncomfortable for both men and horses." Warmer spring weather brought active campaigning, and the Tenth spent much of the year tangling with Rebel forces at a myriad of geographical locations with exotic names like Bull's Gap, Mossy Creek and Strawberry Plains. The unit's first "serious" engagement involved an intense campaign to capture the strategic East Tennessee and Virginia Railroad bridge over the Watuaga River at Carter's Station, Tennessee. In the first phase of the action on April 25, Major Smith led the Michiganians across open ground under fire and routed the Rebels. The well-defended bridge caused the Yankees to break off the attack, but not before Captain Weatherwax and two other troopers were killed and another sixteen men wounded. Colonel Luther Trowbridge, who later commanded the Tenth and composed the postwar regimental history, felt the skirmish helped the Tenth become a "strong aggressive force." However, Trowbridge mourned the loss of Weatherwax, "a noble man, and a soldier of dauntless courage [whose death] was most deeply felt."[78]

Sergeant Edward Drew, a twenty-five-year-old Kent County soldier, also earned battlefield recognition in late summer fighting. Drew and six fellow troopers defended a river ford, delaying a Rebel brigade for about four hours and inflicting fifty enemy casualties. The badly outnumbered Michiganians surrendered only after being outflanked. An impressed Rebel general commended the Yankees: "If I had 300 such men as you, I could march straight through hell."[79]

Elsewhere on that late August day in 1864, Major Smith led a seventy-two-man scouting party to ascertain enemy strength near a place called

Flat Creek Bridge. In the process, Smith's men routed a four-hundred-man-strong Texas cavalry regiment and took forty prisoners. However, the Rebels recovered and forced the Yankees to beat a hasty retreat. In the process, Lieutenants Robert G. Barr and Jacob Weatherwax (Captain Benjamin Weatherwax's younger brother) and about half of Smith's command were captured. After the Rebels "stripped" the Yankees of their boots and "most of their clothing," they paroled them. The indignant Michiganians made their way back to camp—a distance of twenty-five miles—over rough and stony roads.[80]

Major Smith's setback at Flat Creek Bridge was rare, since the North sent to war few men who sat "taller in the saddle." Israel Smith was born in Grand Rapids shortly after his parents moved from Rhode Island. Educated in private schools

Twenty-two-year-old Jacob Weatherwax entered the Tenth Michigan Cavalry as a first sergeant. Promoted to second lieutenant, he took a disability discharge in late 1864 and returned home to Ottawa County. *Author's collection.*

and at Albion College, Smith also worked in his father's lumbering mill, then studied law before heading west. By 1860, he had returned to Grand Rapids after failing to "strike it rich" in the California gold fields. Smith joined the Third Michigan Infantry as a private in 1861; an officer's commission soon followed. Captain Smith was twice wounded at Second Bull Run. Subsequent staff positions did not prevent Smith from seeing action. At Gettysburg, he rallied troops in the Wheatfield until a wound forced him to leave the field. According to his brigade commander, "Smith saluted me with perfect coolness, expressed to me the regret he felt in not being able to be of further service to me, and went off without hurrying."[81]

Smith never returned to the Third Michigan Infantry but entered the Tenth Michigan Cavalry as a major. In one extensive postwar exposé, Smith's "flying cavalry" saw plenty of action in "nearly every Union expedition that was undertaken in East Tennessee in 1864 and 1865 [including] many skirmishes and minor actions with rebel cavalry." In one late-war action, Smith led a small command armed with Spencer carbines that successfully flanked a much-larger Rebel force and sent them fleeing in confusion. According to one chronicler, Smith and his "gallant band [were] as daring as it proved successful." Given his considerable heroics, it is little wonder that an early 1865 observer noted, "The name of the gallant Major Smith, alone, ought to secure recruits in sufficient numbers" to fill the ranks of the Tenth. By war's end, Smith commanded the Tenth Michigan Cavalry, earning brevet brigadier general honors and accolades from professional soldiers under whom he served. One veteran general claimed Smith's "merits [were] unsurpassed by any officer of [his] acquaintance."[82]

The Tenth saw considerable action during the final days of the war, especially raiding southwestern Virginia. The regimental historian bemoaned the lack of attention the Tenth received for capturing the key Confederate works at Saltville. Shortly after Lee's surrender at Appomattox, the Tenth was ordered south to assist in the capture of the fleeing Confederate president. Jefferson Davis was captured by a different Michigan cavalry regiment, but the Tenth marched more than 1,800 miles during the last two months of the war, often living off the country.[83]

The Tenth Michigan Cavalry served as occupation troops in Tennessee until the unit was mustered out and returned home in mid-November 1865.[84]

First New York Cavalry ("Lincoln Cavalry")

Shortly after the fall of Fort Sumter, some impatient Michiganians joined units from other states rather than wait for the additional call for troops. In one unique case, a company of Grand Rapids men headed east to join another Valley City resident who commanded the First New York Cavalry Regiment.

In 1833, twenty-six-year-old Andrew T. McReynolds arrived in Detroit from his native Ireland. One nineteenth-century historian hailed McReynolds as a man who "took an active part in the political and military history of the state and nation," accruing a record of being the "first in everything." Besides a stint in the Michigan State Senate, McReynolds persuaded President James Polk to commission him a U.S. Army officer during the Mexican War. Serving with Third U.S. Dragoons, Captain McReynolds earned commendations "for gallant and meritorious conduct" at the Battles of Contreras and Cherubusco. At the latter, he suffered a severe wound that left his left arm permanently useless. McReynolds returned to Detroit after the Mexican War but moved to Grand Rapids in 1859.[85]

In the early weeks of the Civil War, New York City patriots approached Philip Kearny, a wealthy New York native with an exceptional martial background, to command a regiment of volunteer cavalry. Kearny had already accepted an offer to command New Jersey troops and recommended the organizers seek out Andrew McReynolds, whom Kearny had met during the Mexican War. When contacted, McReynolds immediately accepted the offer and left for New York City. Described as "a little below the medium stature, and solidly built, with a broad, smooth face" and shoulder-length hair, McReynolds also received his commission directly from President Lincoln—a distinct rarity. As a result of the president's interest in volunteer cavalry, the regiment was dubbed the First Lincoln Cavalry, with recruits coming from an assortment of groups—the city's upper class, German immigrants and even distant Michigan. On September 3, 1861, the Grand Rapids Company, commanded by Captain Anson N. Norton, joined the First Lincoln Cavalry in Washington, D.C., as Company K. The regimental historian described the Michiganians as "mostly stalwart Western men." When homesickness became an early war problem, Erastus W. Noble, a twenty-five-year-old from Grand Rapids, used his musical talents and composed a number of verses "touching in a humorous way" on the men's strengths. Noble's efforts soon had the men "heartily singing and making merry over their hardships." According to regimental historian William Harrison Beach, Noble's compositions helped Company K become some of the regiment's "best men."[86]

On a bright and beautiful morning in late August 1861, "a vast multitude" assembled in and around New York City's Union Square to send the First Lincoln Cavalry off to war. After appropriate speeches, Colonel McReynolds was presented with a magnificent dappled gray horse named Lightfoot. The cavalrymen marched down Broadway "to the hearty cheers from the mass of people" crowding the street and waving flags from "every window." The First Lincoln Cavalry saw service throughout the war in the Washington, D.C. area, including the spring 1862 Peninsula Campaign and the late 1864 Shenandoah Valley Campaign.[87]

One of Colonel McReynolds's more notable command decisions occurred at the Second Battle of Winchester in mid-June 1863. Although the battle was an overwhelming Rebel victory, McReynolds commanded a brigade of Yankee cavalry that successfully eluded capture. In the process, he displayed "coolness, self-possession, courage and the highest judgment" in the face of overwhelming odds. Two weeks later, McReynolds was also credited with initiating a "daring act well done" when his troopers destroyed a key pontoon bridge across the Potomac River, further delaying the Rebel army's retreat following the Battle of Gettysburg.[88]

Colonel McReynolds resigned his commission in June 1864, but his son Benjamin Franklin McReynolds remained with the regiment. The younger McReynolds, who had attended Grand Rapids schools before the war, joined the First Lincoln as a second lieutenant in September 1862. Benjamin McReynolds served as the regimental, brigade and division commissary officer until early 1865, when he was discharged for disability. He had the dubious distinction of attending Ford's Theatre on the evening of April 14, 1865, and witnessing President Lincoln's assassination. McReynolds later recorded, "I had a good opportunity of seeing the tragedy which unfortunately was too real.…When I look back it seems like a dream."[89]

BUILDING BRIDGES AND
ENGINEERING VICTORY

We don't surrender much.
—*Colonel William Powell Innes, First Michigan Engineers and Mechanics*

Their achievements were scattered all across the war-torn South. They built dozens of bridges, from massive trestle bridges to simpler pontoon bridges. They wrecked and repaired miles of railroads. They corduroyed roads, constructed warehouses, operated sawmills, built blockhouses, fixed broken wagons and—on one occasion—devised an unconventional pontoon bridge that saved an army from starving. They rarely saw combat, but on those occasions when they came under fire, they performed admirably. The First Regiment Michigan Engineers and Mechanics, which gained a reputation for efficiency and quality work throughout the war's western theater, had its origins in Grand Rapids.

The creation of a Michigan engineering regiment began during the summer of 1861 when agents arrived in west Michigan seeking recruits for a Chicago-based volunteer engineering regiment. William Coffinberry, a civil engineer, and Barker Borden, an architect, builder and contractor, were raising a company for that unit, when they sat down with fellow Grand Rapids businessmen James W. Sligh, a merchant and local militia officer, and Perrin V. Fox, a contractor and bridge builder. They determined Michigan needed its own engineering regiment. Although skilled in their respective trades, these men lacked the influence or prestige to gain the needed authorization to organize such a unit. Instead, they approached William Powell Innes and successfully convinced him to "take hold of the matter."[90]

Well known throughout the state, the thirty-year-old Innes had migrated to Grand Rapids from his native New York in 1853. Before the war, he had supervised the construction of an assortment of railroads, most notably the Detroit and Milwaukee Railroad, which stretched from Detroit to Grand Haven. With twenty years of engineering experience, Innes wired the secretary of war asking if the Federal government would accept a regiment of Michigan engineers. Secretary of War Simon Cameron approved if Governor Austin Blair supported the concept. Blair eagerly authorized the unit's formation, pledged his complete assistance in the endeavor and immediately traveled to Grand Rapids to meet with the organizers and Grand Rapids mayor Wilder D. Foster. On September 13, Michigan adjutant general Jonathan Robertson issued the necessary orders. In a few days of swift action, the First Michigan Engineers and Mechanics had become a reality—at least on paper.[91]

A well-known and respected railroad engineer, the thirty-two-year-old William Powell Innes of Grand Rapids was the unanimous choice to command the First Michigan Engineers and Mechanics. In March 1865, he was promoted to brevet brigadier general "for gallant and efficient service." *From Sligh,* First Engineers and Mechanics.

Blair appointed Innes colonel, and recruiting began in earnest. Four of the regiment's ten companies were filled with men from Kent County. Regimental founders Borden, Coffinberry, Fox and Sligh commanded these companies (B, C, D and F, respectively) as captains. Herman Palmerlee, also from Grand Rapids, commanded Company I. Ionia, Albion, Kalamazoo, Jackson and Marshall furnished additional companies. Grand Rapids men among the line officers included Surgeon William H. DeCamp and Quartermaster Robert S. Innes. A native New Yorker, Dr. DeCamp had graduated from the Medical College of Geneva (New York) and migrated to Grand Rapids in 1853. Innes was a cartographer, engineer and Colonel Innes's younger brother.[92]

These four Grand Rapids artisans (Wright L. Coffinberry, Baker Borden, Perrin V. Fox and James Sligh) led the campaign to organize the First Michigan Engineers and Mechanics— one of the war's unique commands. *From Sligh,* First Engineers and Mechanics.

As historian Mark Hoffman chronicles in *My Brave Mechanics*, "[A]t least half of the original recruits were skilled craftsmen or artisans." One in three was a carpenter, joiner or cabinetmaker. The men had extensive experience in carriage or wagon making, repairing wheels, blacksmithing and railroad construction. The regiment's many farmers understood how to clear a forest. The average age for the engineers was almost twenty-nine—about three years older than the average Northern volunteer.[93]

Since Camp Anderson in Grand Rapids already hosted the formation and training of two regiments of cavalry (Second and Third), the First Engineers moved to Marshall. Located at the Calhoun County Fairgrounds, "Camp Owen" remained the Engineers' home for the next three months. Delays in securing engineering tools and uniforms led to understandable frustration and prevented the First Engineers from leaving for the front as early as Colonel Innes had hoped.[94]

On October 10, 1861, an estimated ten thousand people flocked to Camp Owen to watch the regiment receive its colors. The ceremony began with a review by Governor Blair. Francis W. Sherman, on behalf of the citizens of Marshall, presented the regiment with a beautiful silk flag, declaring:

> *Its mission is to be borne, and to float over the heads of your gallant men, wherever the fate of war may lead them. Its mission, under God and your bravery, is to participate in the salvation of our country from the armed attacks of rebellious traitors, to aid in the maintenance of our free institutions and our glorious constitution and in the preservation of our national Union.*[95]

Lieutenant Colonel Kinsman A. Hunton of Marshall, filling in for Colonel Innes, who was in Washington, confidently predicted that "in future years," the name of the First Regiment of Michigan Engineers "shall be found recorded among the honored brave." The Engineers mustered into federal service on October 29 and left Marshall six weeks later. All along the way to Louisville, Kentucky, enthusiastic receptions greeted the Engineers. As one Michiganian noted, "Everybody came out to see us from the aged to the infant."[96]

The Engineers were excited to go to war, but two contentious issues generated problems. First, the troops were offended when issued "good for nothing" Prussian muskets. A much greater problem was an earlier promise the men would receive an engineer's pay of seventeen dollars a month versus the standard infantryman's pay of thirteen dollars a month. One Grand

Rapids soldier cautioned, "We have been having a flare-up in our regiment and I don't know how it will come out." Weeks later, the same soldier predicted, "The boys are going to bolt on the account of our pay." Colonel Innes's promise of higher pay had never been authorized, and congressional debate on the matter bogged down over fears about establishing a precedent for thousands of men building railroads in the private sector. Eventually, the temporary drama was resolved, and the engineers received the higher salary. At the same time, two new companies were added. For most of the war, Companies L and M served independently of the regiment.[97]

The Engineers were divided into four detachments of two and three companies each and distributed throughout Kentucky to maximize use of their skills over a wide area. Companies D and F (both heavily recruited in Kent County), as well as Company G, joined General George Thomas's division in eastern Kentucky. In late January, these Michiganians were camped near the rear of the Union position when the Rebels attacked. The Engineers did not see action in the decisive Rebel defeat at Mill Springs, but Captain Sligh noted the Michiganians had repaired roads that allowed Union reinforcements to prevent Thomas's division from being "cut to pieces." Thomas credited the Engineers with being "the best looking body of men on the Ground, and the quietest and best regulated camp under his charge." A beaming Captain Sligh added, "We intend that the future will find us equal to the present." However, the Michiganians also had the depressing task of gathering the wounded and burying the dead. As one Engineer recorded, "It was the most sickening sight I have ever seen."[98]

In April 1862, eight Engineer companies, under the command of Colonel Innes, left Nashville with General Don Carol Buell's Army of the Ohio to join General U.S. Grant's Army of the Tennessee at Pittsburg Landing on the Tennessee River. On this march, the Engineers built several sturdy bridges, allowing Buell's army to reinforce Grant's army sooner as it tangled with Rebel forces at the Battle of Shiloh. The Engineers missed the fight, but in viewing the carnage of the war's first bloody battle, Captain Sligh agonized that the battlefield was "literally a graveyard." After Shiloh, the Engineers played an active role in the siege of the important railroad junction of Corinth, Mississippi, by constructing miles of corduroy roads through the swamps. After days of constant work, Albert Graves, a Kent County sergeant, explained, "We have been constantly on detail for opening roads for the army to advance…much of the way through swamps and low land full of brooks which had to be bridged." After the Yankees captured Corinth in late May, the Engineers followed the Tennessee River

Twenty-four-year-old Edward H. Clark of Grand Rapids joined the army in late 1861 and served four years with the First Michigan Engineers. *Courtesy of Dave Broene.*

into Alabama, building bridges, repairing track and running trains. The Engineers' accomplishments garnered recognition. According to one Michigan newspaper account, "[N]o regiment in the service has been of more use to the government" than the First Engineers. When General Buell left the Army of the Ohio in late 1862, he complimented Colonel Innes for his regiment's "efficient services."[99]

By October 1862, the Engineers were once again divided into contingents. One detachment (Companies A, C and H) under Major Enos Hopkins saw action at the Battle of Perryville. At a key moment late in the battle, the Engineers were rushed forward from the rear ranks to block a Rebel advance. Hopkins exhorted his battalion forward by declaring, "Now my brave mechanics if you work you can fight, follow me." The engineers slowed but did not stop the Rebel surge. By evening, the Michiganians had suffered fourteen wounded, two fatally, and several more captured or missing. Hopkins's men expected more fighting in the morning, but the Rebels withdrew during the night. Hopkins's battalion performed well despite the fact none had ever "seen the elephant."[100]

In late December 1862, a consolidated First Michigan Engineers bivouacked near Nashville soon distinguished themselves in ways nobody would have anticipated. As the Battle of Stones River raged near Murfreesboro, the Engineers were ordered to guard the army's supply train by moving to La Vergne, located between Murfreesboro and Nashville. After reaching the small village—and aware that Rebel raiders moved through the area—Colonel Innes strengthened the defenses of his new position. Soon after the breastworks were completed, Rebels from General Joseph Wheeler's four-thousand-man command swept into town. The Engineers mustered about four hundred men and soon faced a series of enemy assaults. Throughout the fight, Rebel sharpshooters and cannons kept the Yankees under "a constant fire." As Innes moved about encouraging his men, a Rebel closed on the colonel, only to be shot down before he could bring his carbine to bear. During the several-hour skirmish, the Rebels sent a flag of truce demanding surrender. Innes roared, "We don't surrender much." A second courier followed, once again demanding the Yankees surrender. An irritated Innes sent the courier packing with a message that if the Rebels sent another courier he would shoot him as a spy. The *Detroit Free Press* later reported:

The scene was at times thrilling beyond description. The rebel horde, exasperated at the successful resistance of the little force, dashed their horses against the circular brush fence, which was only breast high, with infuriated shouts and curses....But the Michigan troops were cool and determined; they loaded fast and aimed well, and, as the troopers rushed on upon all sides, they were met with staggering volleys almost at the muzzle of the muskets.[101]

After seven failed attacks, the Rebels gave up, leaving fifty dead on the battlefield, whom the Engineers later buried. The stubborn Michiganians suffered one killed and six wounded. Despite later-day claims, the Engineers had failed to save any wagons or protect any supplies. However, their heroic stand against overwhelming odds received national recognition and "became the single incident most associated with Innes and the Michigan Engineers." The influential *New York Tribune* expressed disappointment in the Union army's performance at Stones River, but editor Horace Greeley congratulated the Engineers for providing a "silver lining to this cloud [by their] most gallant defense" at La Vergne. After the battle, General William S. Rosecrans praised the Engineers for their gallant stand, while the *Detroit Free Press* added, "Truly this was one of the most gallant affairs of the campaign." The accolades proved satisfying to Innes, but a more rewarding experience came in the Engineers' camp that night when a group of men led by Grand Rapids sergeant Charles T. Wooding hoisted the colonel on their shoulders and carried him around the camp chanting, "We don't surrender much."[102]

During the summer of 1863, the Engineers constructed one of its most impressive works—a trestle rail bridge over Tennessee's Elk River. Rebel forces had destroyed the existing bridge, disrupting the supply line to Nashville. The repair operation had been tasked to the Pioneer Brigade—three battalions of men with engineering responsibilities commanded by a West Point honor graduate. The Pioneers argued such a bridge would take up to six weeks to complete. When a frustrated General Rosecrans sought a second opinion,

Colonel Innes promised a bridge in eight days—provided he kept the Pioneer Brigade away. Rosecrans acquiesced. A week later, the Engineers completed an impressive structure that stood 470 feet long and 58 feet high. Soon after the Elk River bridge opened, the Engineers built a 350-foot-long bridge over the nearby Duck River. According to regimental historian Sligh, "The building of these bridges in the short space of time in which they were accomplished was among the remarkable engineering achievements of the war and brought the highest commendations from the commanding generals." A few months later, the Engineers used their considerable skills to save an army in serious trouble.[103]

Following the late September 1863 Battle of Chickamauga, the defeated Army of the Cumberland retreated into Chattanooga, Tennessee, where it soon faced a siege. The situation worsened as Rebel guns atop the nearby heights closed the Yankees' primary supply route on the Tennessee River. Supplies did arrive via an alternative route that covered twice the distance and over terrible terrain. Mules died by the hundreds, and their carcasses littered the trail. Even more serious than coping with dead mules, the Army of the Cumberland was running out of food and hope.[104]

General Rosecrans turned to Captain Perrin Fox, who commanded a battalion of First Michigan Engineers (Companies D and K) at Chattanooga, to seek a way to alleviate the worsening supply crisis. Despite a shortage of suitable lumber, Fox designed a workable pontoon, albeit an unorthodox one. The Pioneer Brigade commander ridiculed Fox's boat, while a more confident Rosecrans told the Michiganians to proceed. Fox's men built two prototypes, which Rosecrans personally tested for buoyancy and stability. "The boats are all right," the general declared. "Go ahead with your work." Completing the boats proved a challenge, forcing the Engineers to operate an area sawmill while scrounging and improvising needed supplies. (Couriers brought nails in their saddlebags, while local cotton sufficed for caulking.) The Michiganians then completed a one-thousand-foot-long pontoon bridge north of the city in two days—a project the Pioneer Brigade had bumbled. Fox assumed more responsibility as his command expanded with the addition of two more Engineering companies (commanded by Captains James D. Robinson and John W. McCrath, both from Grand Rapids). After arriving in Chattanooga and assuming overall command, General U.S. Grant approved a bold plan from General William F. Smith, the army's new engineering officer, to build another pontoon bridge west of the city at a place called Brown's Ferry. There was one problem—the ferry was on the south side of the

The Elk River Bridge—built in eight days in south-central Tennessee—served as one of the more spectacular accomplishments of the Michigan Engineers. Officers standing in the right foreground include Surgeon William H. De Camp, Captain James W. Sligh and Adjutant Charles W. Calkins, all of Grand Rapids. *From Sligh,* First Engineers and Mechanics.

river and in enemy hands. Smith turned to Fox, giving him seventy-two hours to convert fifty boats into landing craft capable of carrying riflemen and collect all the necessary materials to build the second bridge. General Montgomery Meigs, the Union army's quartermaster general, watched the Michigan Engineers with fascination, sending detailed reports of their work to Secretary of War Edwin Stanton. When Smith's deadline expired, Fox had achieved the general's goal.[105]

During the early morning hours of October 27, Fox's Engineers, aided by one hundred men from the Twenty-First Michigan Infantry commanded by Captain Benton D. Fox (Lowell), loaded bridge-laying supplies in wagons. After traversing the miserable road across a peninsula called Moccasin Point, the Engineers reached the north bank of the river opposite Brown's Ferry. At the same time, other Engineers piloted the recently constructed pontoon boats and two additional rafts loaded with Yankee infantrymen down the Tennessee River. Taking advantage of the fog and darkness, the bluecoats covered the seven miles in two hours, landing at Brown's Ferry—much to the surprise of Rebel pickets. As the bluecoats secured a bridgehead, Fox's command started laying the pontoon bridge. Despite

Rebel shells "falling thick and fast all around" them, the Yankees finished the 870-foot bridge in less than eight hours.[106]

The Brown's Ferry bridge, nicknamed the "Michigan Bridge," opened up the "Cracker Line," which spelled relief for the besieged Union army. The Cracker Line ran from Bridgeport, Alabama, to Kelly's Ford on the Tennessee River. At the ford, the supply line left the river and moved by road to Brown's Ferry. The route also allowed considerable Union reinforcements to cross at Brown's Ferry on their way to Chattanooga. Less than a month later, well-supplied Yankees stormed the heights surrounding the city and routed the Rebel army. General George Thomas, who replaced Rosecrans as commander of the Army of the Cumberland, described the opening of the Cracker Line as "brilliant." Back home in Michigan, the *Detroit Free Press* hailed the achievement as "a feat unparalleled in the history of pontooning." General Smith focused his "highest praise" on Captain Fox's "vigorous and skillful superintendence." Even years after the war, Smith charged that without "without the zealous and efficient labors of Captain Fox…the bridge could not have been made or thrown." More recently, historian James McDonough concluded in his seminal work on the Chattanooga Campaign, "Once in a great while, and perhaps when least expected, the awful drama of war narrows to a very small focus, to a relative handful of men, and the story of a great struggle takes a decisive turn through the successful execution of a simple, daring plan."[107]

Those closest to Captain Fox knew he would not fail. Described by one Michigan officer after the war as "a very prince of men—with six feet of bones, sinew and brains," Fox also was a champion wrestler in the Army of the Cumberland. According to a fellow Grand Rapids officer serving in the Twenty-First Michigan Infantry, Fox faced a challenge from another Yankee—a Wisconsin Swede who stood six feet, six inches tall and weighed 240 pounds. A newly crafted amphitheater that included reserved seats for high-ranking officers featured the much-anticipated match between the two midwestern warriors. Despite the size difference, Fox won easily, sending the Swede's backers straggling to their camps "hatless, coatless and moneyless," according to one observer. To assuage their disappointment, the losers claimed Fox stood seven feet tall and weighed over 300 pounds. Acclaimed as the "most talked about man in the army," Captain Fox's fame as an engineering officer paled, according to one sympathetic observer, "when compared to the glory won in the gladiator's ring."[108]

Tragedy struck the Engineers in late 1863. On October 23, a train carrying Captain Sligh and a small detail that included assistant surgeon

Above: Michigan Engineers who played a significant role in the late 1863 Yankee victory at Chattanooga, Tennessee, included Captain John W. McCrath and his Company B, pictured here. McCrath of Grand Rapids served in the army from September 1861 through September 1865. *From Sligh*, First Engineers and Mechanics.

Left: Captain James D. Robinson and fellow Grand Rapids soldiers from his Company C, First Michigan Engineers, were among the many victorious Yankees who posed on Lookout Mountain, Tennessee, in late 1863. The thirty-nine-year-old Robinson went to war as a first lieutenant in late 1861 and mustered out four years later. *From Sligh*, First Engineers and Mechanics.

Henry Van Ostrand, also from Grand Rapids, derailed a few miles south of Tullahoma, Tennessee. Rebel raiders had sabotaged the tracks and attacked the train after it ran off the rails. Sligh lay pinned under the wreckage. Van Ostrand returned to Tullahoma for assistance, securing two Engineer companies who drove off the Rebels. The delay in getting Sligh to a hospital may not have mattered. The badly injured captain died three weeks later, becoming the regiment's only officer to die in service. His remains were brought back to Grand Rapids. After an elegiac eulogy, the *Grand Rapids Record Eagle* hoped "the turf be ever green over the grave of the fallen patriot."[109]

James W. Sligh, a Grand Rapids merchant and a prewar militia member, joined the First Engineers and commanded a company. A train wreck orchestrated by Rebel saboteurs led to Sligh's death in late 1863. *From Sligh, First Engineers and Mechanics.*

After the Brown's Ferry project, several engineering companies remained in Chattanooga operating sawmills, crafting railroad ties and constructing various defenses, while several other companies pursued similar projects in southeastern Tennessee and northern Alabama. From June to the end of September 1864, most Engineers focused on protecting Sherman's supply line as his army moved toward Atlanta. The summer also coincided with the end of the Engineers' three-year enlistments. Many men reenlisted, but not Colonel Innes. Innes chose to leave the service for a variety of reasons, including a tendency to become "embroiled in controversy" outside the regiment. According to historian Hoffman, Innes "might have been his own worst enemy," with a propensity to be on the "losing side" of too many disputes. In a farewell to the regiment he had created, Innes told the Engineers, "The readiness with which you answered to your Country's call gave proof of your true patriotism." Hoping the war would end soon, Innes reminded the men, "Our Country's flag must float over not a part of but the whole land, with its stripes untarnished and its stars undimmed." As the war ended, Innes earned a promotion to brevet brigadier general.[110]

Eighteen-year-old John Thibos of Grand Rapids mustered into the First Michigan Engineers in late 1863 and mustered out in September 1865. *Courtesy of the State Archives of Michigan.*

Major John B. Yates of Ionia assumed command of the Engineers, who assisted in the destruction of Atlanta. At the urging of Captain Orlando M. Poe, Sherman's chief engineer, the Michigan Engineers prepared to join the Yankee march across Georgia. First, the Engineers destroyed Atlanta's railroads and anything that might be of use to the enemy. According to regimental historian Sligh, "The sky was bright with fires from burning buildings," as the Engineers were among the last Union troops to leave the city's smoking ruins behind. Attached directly to Sherman's headquarters, the Engineers' primary role during the four-week excursion consisted largely of destroying railroads. However, the men also repaired roads, built corduroy roads and laid pontoon bridges. Their reputation preceded them. One high-ranking general admitted he did not need "all the engineer troops," but he "earnestly" hoped to have "at least one company of the First Michigan" added to his command. Notwithstanding all the hard work, the Engineers agreed it was pleasant service: "[W]e had fun" crossing Georgia.[111]

Once Savannah was captured, the Engineers improved the city's defenses before Sherman's army pushed into South Carolina. Once again, the Engineers spent most of their time destroying railroads or corduroying roads across the low and swampy Carolina countryside. On March 19, 1865, as Sherman's army neared Goldsboro, North Carolina, the Rebels struck. Colonel Yates advanced his men toward the sound of gunfire and ordered them to dig in. The Engineers remained dug in for a few days but did not see any fighting in the Battle of Bentonville. When the Rebel threat ended, the Yankees entered Goldsboro, where all twelve companies of the First Michigan Engineers were reunited for the first time. After a few restful days, one veteran Engineer anticipated taking part "in the grand final overthrow of the great rebellion." But the war was ending quickly, and news of the surrender of Lee's army at Appomattox "almost made the boys crazy by the way they cheered and yelled." Rebel forces soon surrendered in North Carolina.[112]

The fighting had ceased, but the Engineers still had work to do getting Sherman's army to the nation's capital. Building a 740-foot-long bridge across the Roanoke River was among the most demanding tasks. Almost three weeks after leaving Raleigh, the Engineers reached Alexandria, Virginia, after "a very hard march." The two-day Grand Review proved rewarding, and Lieutenant Sligh remembered bouquets of flowers showered on the victors and an abundance of handkerchiefs "waving a welcome." Some Engineers arrived home in mid-June, while newer enlistees served out their enlistment in Louisville, Kentucky. On October 12, 1865, Walter Phillips, who joined the service at Grand Rapids in late 1863 at the age of twenty-four, was the last member of the First Engineers to be discharged.[113]

6

EARNING THE RIGHT
TO BE CALLED VETERANS

Men of known endurance and courage…bummer[s] would put up a stronger fight for a general assortment of plantation provisions than a whole regiment would from pure patriotism and love of country.
—Captain Charles E. Belknap, Twenty-First Michigan Infantry

All of Ionia turned out on September 8, 1862—mustering day for the newly organized Twenty-First Michigan Infantry. Composed mainly of men from the Grand River valley, the Twenty-First was part of Michigan's response (eight new regiments) to President Lincoln's latest call for troops. Three of the regiment's ten companies (B, E and H) came from the Grand Rapids area. Recruiting began in early July, and new enlistees gathered at "Camp Sigel" outside of Ionia. Among the field officers, assistant surgeon Dr. Charles R. Perry of Lowell lived the closest to Grand Rapids. The regiment's oldest member was fifty-six-year-old James Heffron of Cannonsburg. Fifteen-year-old Charles E. Belknap was among the youngest recruits. A native New Yorker whose family moved to Grand Rapids in 1854, Belknap enlisted with his mother's permission, as long as he promised to avoid using tobacco, drinking whiskey or playing cards. (His father already served in the Eighth Michigan Infantry.) The younger Belknap's impressive military career began when his company elected him "fourth" sergeant even before the regiment left Michigan. The Twenty-First also boasted sixty-three pairs of brothers, including the Newsons of Caledonia: nineteen-year-old James and eighteen-year-old Horace, who were joined by their forty-one-year-old father, William.[114]

In late August, the 1,008-man Twenty-First Michigan received its uniforms, Model 1854 Austrian Lorenz rifles and miscellaneous accouterments. However, the Rebel invasion of Kentucky created an emergency, cutting short the training time at Camp Sigel. A festive day followed the formal mustering ceremonies as proud friends and relatives gathered there to watch the oath of allegiance and flag presentation ceremonies. A banquet and the presentation of gifts to various officers followed speakers that included U.S. Senator Zach. ah Chandler. Captain James Cavanaugh, commander of the Grand Rapids Company, received a "handsome and costly sash, belt and revolver." The exciting day ended with a dress parade. Fifty years after the war, one veteran recalled, "[O]ur dreams were of terrific fighting, heroic action and glory."[115]

When the Twenty-First Michigan headed to the Ionia train station early on the morning of September 10, the men enjoyed a prepared breakfast and a large crowd ready to send them off to war. After riding in boxcars to Detroit (passenger cars were unavailable), the men encountered cheering, smiling crowds offering baskets of food. The Ionia Cornet Band, which accompanied the regiment to Detroit, added patriotic tunes. As the regiment headed toward Cincinnati, enthusiastic Ohioans greeted them all along the way.[116]

After the Twenty-First Michigan crossed into Kentucky and joined General Don Carlos Buell's Army of the Ohio, soldiering dramatically changed. The physical demands exceeded anything the men had experienced as civilians. Long marches—up to sixteen hours on some days—intense heat and shortages of water and food led one veteran to recall "stopping at midday by the side of the road to eat salt pork and hardtack from unwashed hands with the dust so thick that men in the ranks would not be able to recognize the comrades with whom they touched shoulders."[117]

One month after leaving Michigan, the men found themselves engaged in the biggest battle ever fought in Kentucky. Although the Michiganians played a minor role in the Battle of Perryville, the Twenty-First "saw the elephant," suffering twenty-four wounded, one mortally, while earning accolades for its "truly commendable" behavior. These Michiganians also confronted other horrors of war after visiting a nearby field hospital. Marcus Bates of Kelloggsville recorded, "[T]he sight, far too revolting to mention here, initiated me into the aftermath of battle, never to be forgotten." Conversely, Sanford Lyon, a twenty-four-year-old Grand Rapids sergeant, expressed confidence and optimism in a letter home: "We have been exposed to the danger of battle and already feel like boyish veterans....[We] recount

Twenty-one-year-old Milo Baxter of Cascade joined the Twenty-First Michigan Infantry in August 1862. He later transferred to the Veterans Reserve Corps, leaving federal service in July 1865. *Courtesy of the State Archives of Michigan.*

our many conflicts on the battlefield till our campfires burn low." Written one week after Perryville, Lyon could not anticipate the horrors that lay ahead.[118]

In the weeks following Perryville, the Twenty-First Michigan discovered the South, which left them unimpressed. Henry Tracy described Perryville as "the most desolate looking county that you have ever saw in your life." Having seen only two schoolhouses in Kentucky, the nineteen-year-old Grand Rapids private concluded local residents must be illiterate. Tracy also noticed Kentuckians often lived in log cabins and the women lacked social graces, especially those who chewed tobacco. According to regimental historian James Genco, in *Into the Tornado of War*, the regiment's time in Kentucky had been "a prolonged period of physical suffering that had no parallel in any subsequent campaign." A month after Perryville, the Twenty-First Michigan traded the desolation they found in Kentucky for a pleasant campsite near Nashville. The army's new commander, William S. Rosecrans, also impressed Quartermaster Sergeant Bates, who claimed that "every soldier came to admire 'General Rosey.'"[119]

The Michiganians also introduced themselves to foraging—a practice that posed a dilemma for officers who struggled with how much stealing to tolerate. Private Tracy noted that the men "generally take whatever [they] can get, that is if [they] don't get caught at it by the officers." On one occasion, Captain Jacob Ferris (Ionia) and Lieutenant Benton Fox (Lowell) led men from Companies B and G to reconnoiter a large brick house of a known slaveholder. A day earlier, the Yankees had seen Rebel cavalrymen there, but on this day, all was quiet. The Yankees delighted in the discovery of a large number of turkeys, leaving one witty Michiganian to boast surviving "a good skirmish [where they] took a good many prisoners." Along with an abundance of "liberated" apples, these Yankees had the fixings for a Thanksgiving feast.[120]

Several weeks later, General Rosecrans advanced his army eastward toward Murfreesboro, Tennessee. The Yankees dealt with freezing temperatures and sheets of rain, followed by sleet and snow that turned the roads into quagmires. Bivouacking in saturated fields deepened the misery. William E. Thornton, a nineteen-year-old Grand Rapids sergeant, described the opening clash with General Braxton Bragg's Rebel army on December 31:

> *The fog had begun to clear away, the rain had ceased for some hours, when some twenty rods to our right and a little to the rear appeared the Confederate force advancing in close ranks, with columns deep with colors and guidons flying, and as they came on…*[with] *a yell sufficient to raise the dead lying on the field in our rear.*[121]

Part of General Philip Sheridan's division, the Twenty-First Michigan experienced some of the fiercest fighting in the bloody Battle of Stones River. Throughout the morning, the Michiganians "made their most gallant stand of the day." One veteran recalled, "Scarcely a man in the regiment came out of the wood without bearing marks of the bullets on his person or clothes." The fighting ended with darkness. According to the historian Genco, "Stones River was a defining event" for the Twenty-First. Suffering 143 casualties (from about 400 men present for duty), the men of the Twenty-First Michigan clearly earned the right to be called "veterans."[122]

Eighteen-year-old William E. Thornton of Grand Rapids mustered into the Twenty-First Michigan Infantry as a sergeant in July 1862. Wounded at the Battle of Stones River, Tennessee, Thornton later earned a promotion to first lieutenant. He resigned his commission in late 1864. *Courtesy of Dave Broene.*

Following months of inactivity, Rosecrans's army slowly advanced toward Chattanooga, Tennessee, during the late summer of 1863. The Yankees successfully forced the Rebels back into Georgia. But the Southerners returned, seeking vengeance, which led to one of the war's bloodiest battles. On the first day of the Battle of Chickamauga, the Twenty-First Michigan heard, but did not see, the fighting. However, few Yankees got any sleep that night knowing the Rebels were close. One Kent County private recorded, "I could hear the rebels in my front talking through the night," while another veteran recalled the evening challenged "the strongest nerves and most courageous hearts."[123]

The Twenty-First Michigan greeted the morning of September 20 near the center of the Union line. At 9:00 a.m., the Sunday quiet was shattered as the "tornado of war" swept across the field occupied by the Michiganians. One Kent County participant recounted the noise proved "so deafening that there was no distinction between artillery and musketry....Dense clouds of smoke marked the lines as it ascended above the tree tops, the very ground trembling beneath the shock as the battle, increasing in fury and volume, gradually approached from the left." In the face of a "perfect storm of lead," according to its commander, the Twenty-First formed a battle-line. The Rebel advance could not be checked, and the Yankee line crumbled. During the melee, the regiment's colonel was wounded and captured and the lieutenant colonel was killed. Major Seymour Chase assumed temporary command.[124]

In the battlefield confusion, a picket detail (thirty men from Company B, led by Lieutenant Albert Barr, a twenty-two-year-old from Grand Rapids, and seven men from Company H, led by seventeen-year-old Lieutenant Charles Belknap, also from Grand Rapids) became separated from the main body. When the Union line collapsed and retreated, this small command was cut off from the Yankee army. The Michiganians repulsed several Rebel attacks, then sought protection in the nearby woods as the graycoats regrouped. Other Yankees joined the beleaguered Michiganians, but the bluecoats remained badly outnumbered. One Kent County private remembered, "We are now cut off from joining our regiment and the rebels are following us so fast that the bullets are coming like hail, some going through our clothing....We had to turn and face their terrible fire." The temporary protection afforded by the trees "didn't last long for they were soon torn to pieces by their cannons which scattered pieces in every direction." Despite pressure on their front and flanks, the Yankees proved a formidable obstacle. One survivor noted, "Our revolving rifles were so hot we could not hold them in our hands." The youthful Belknap directed men with one hand while discharging his revolver with the other. A postwar account recalled how his "coolness and matchless audacity and bravery inspired his comrades to fight with even greater fury."[125]

Relief arrived, and the Rebels finally fell back, although some of the Yankees left their protective cover and chased the Rebels—albeit briefly. The

Seymour Chase of Cannonsburg started his military service as a thirty-nine-year-old captain of Company H, Twenty-First Michigan Infantry. Promoted to major in early 1863, he earned commendations for leading his regiment at the Battle of Chickamauga "with signal efficiency and bravery." Chase resigned his commission for reasons of disability in October 1863. *Courtesy of the State Archives of Michigan.*

pickets made an orderly withdrawal and soon rejoined the Twenty-First. According to historian Genco, "[T]he struggle around the Widow Glenn's house proved an important part of the battle, delaying and disrupting the Confederate onslaught and buying precious time for General Thomas to organize his heroic stand on Snodgrass Hill." Major Chase commended the picket detachment for their "special gallantry." The forty-year-old Chase, a Cannonsburg resident who had gone to war as captain of Company H, was hailed as "a man of superior judgment and excellence of character." Keeping the regiment together during its retreat earned Chase commendations from his brigade commander for "signal efficiency and bravery." The Twenty-First Michigan entered the Battle of Chickamauga three hundred strong and suffered losses of eleven killed, fifty-eight wounded, thirty-eight missing and three captured.[126]

For the year following Chickamauga, the Twenty-First Michigan, now commanded by Colonel Loomis K. Bishop of Cannonsburg (after Chase's resignation), worked with army engineers constructing bridges, buildings and hospitals before joining Sherman's March to the Sea. In November 1864, the regiment left Atlanta, now commanded by Major Benton Fox (Lowell), an officer who enjoyed "widespread popularity" among his men.

Generally dry weather, level marching terrain, an absence of enemy troops and an abundance of corn, sweet potatoes and sorghum explain why one Ionia officer recounted the month-long march across Georgia as "the most delightful part of all our military experience."[127]

To keep the Northern army fed, Sherman's "bummers" efficiently executed liberal foraging throughout the countryside. To prevent bummers from overlapping their efforts or running into one another, some brigades created special one-hundred-man foraging units with each regiment contributing twenty-five men. Eighteen-year-old Captain Belknap commanded his brigade's foraging unit. Years after the war, Belknap described the bummers' tasks: "Foraging and fighting anything and everything that came [their] way, picking up rebel stragglers and deserters, hunting out the roads, and acting as scouts and guides." Foragers might be gone a few days and travel miles from the main Yankee columns. According to one Michigan officer, foragers acted as a "broom from forty to sixty miles in width that swept the country clean of cattle, pigs, horses, mules, sweet potatoes, corn, bacon, ham, and generally all property of any use to a moving army." An Ionia officer characterized the typical bummer as possessing "a character full of good humor and the milk of human kindness, but with a soul sternly set upon the duty of despoiling the country." A discerning Belknap reflected on his experience after the war, claiming that "a Bummer would put up a stronger fight for a general assortment of plantation provisions than a whole regiment would from pure patriotism and love of country." This work "called [for] the best men from the ranks; men of known endurance and courage." Although under orders not to confiscate private property, it happened. Frequently, Georgians in the path of the advancing Union army buried their valuables in a futile attempt to deceive the bummers. As Belknap noted, "With untiring zeal the foragers prodded the ground with ramrod and bayonet. It was certainly comical to see these military agriculturalists punching the unoffending earth in an apparently idiotic way."[128]

Occasionally, the bummer experience had nothing to do with feeding an army. One day, Belknap's men happened across two abandoned girls, ages three and five. Dressed in rags and filthy, the girls repeatedly said, "Mamma gone." The Yankees bathed the orphans and found them new clothes. Efforts to find their family or anyone who knew them failed. Eventually, a wounded officer took them to Michigan. A postwar search yielded no leads, and according to Belknap, "[T]he mystery was never solved." On another raiding foray, Belknap discovered a woman alone in child labor. Totally inexperienced in the birthing process, the young captain did not panic. He rode two miles to the camp, recruited a father, returned to the plantation and helped deliver a healthy baby.[129]

The occupation of Savannah in the days prior to Christmas allowed Belknap's bummers to bring some much-needed holiday cheer to one desperate Georgia town. Loading up one hundred mules with bread, pork, coffee and sugar, Belknap commanded a ninety-man expedition to a nearby village ravaged by war. Along the way, Belknap even led his homesick men in the singing of Christmas carols. After the festive procession reached its destination, the men built a makeshift corral for their animals, prepared fires and started frying pork and boiling coffee. As curious local residents peeked out of their homes, Belknap explained, "Uncle Sam is not making war upon women and children and has sent us

In mid-1862, underage Charles Belknap successfully joined the Twenty-First Michigan Infantry Regiment. Belknap's wartime career rivaled his notable postwar achievements, which included serving as Grand Rapids mayor, a U.S. congressman and an enthusiastic student of history. *Author's collection.*

with the best he had in store that you may have a Christmas dinner and will fill your tables with enough to carry them over until you can be cared for in other ways." The next morning, the Yankees distributed the remaining supplies of food before heading back to Savannah.[130]

Miserable weather greeted the Yankees as they marched north into South Carolina. One Kent County soldier recorded in his diary, "We have had very bad luck today. The roads are so bad that it is almost impossible for man or beast to move." In some cases, the men, horses and wagons struggled through waist-deep mud. Most days, the Rebels were at best an annoyance—at least until March 19, 1865, near Bentonville, North Carolina. A day earlier, Belknap's ninety-man bummer force moved out early, "tired, sore, cross and ugly." At dawn the next day, the Yankees ran into a much larger Rebel force. Belknap's men flanked the enemy position, discovering in the process that they faced a considerably larger enemy force. Belknap reported his discovery, but the Union high command refused to believe the reports, convinced the Rebels only represented a rear guard. At the same time, the Twenty-First Michigan led its brigade into an area of thick woods, tangled underbrush and swamps that obscured the advancing Rebel line. The Yankees fell back "exposed in the open field with enemy artillery and musketry pouring in from the front and flanks." Captain Arthur C. Prince, a Grand Rapids veteran who started the war as a sergeant and now commanded the Twenty-First, reported, "The enemy proving too much for us [and] we were obliged to fall back." But poor positioning posed a challenge for the Twenty-First as it retreated down a ravine. As the Rebels overwhelmed the Yankee position, the chaplain of the Twenty-First recalled, "We were in an uncomfortable and tite [sic] place…[as] the contest grew more intense every moment." Captain Prince later added, "Before we could complete [the breastworks] the enemy charged upon us, and being of greater strength turned both flanks." With enemy fire coming from the front and both flanks, the Twenty-First's retreat changed into a rout. Lieutenant Charles Sears (Courtland Township, Kent County), who had enlisted in 1862 as a corporal, waited until the last of the regiment and its colors had left the field before retreating to the rear. Badly bloodied, the Twenty-First was placed in reserve for the remainder of the battle.[131]

As the morning worsened for the Twenty-First Michigan, Belknap's Bummers fought "their own private engagement" elsewhere on the battlefield. Belknap made it safely back to Union lines and, over the course of the next several days, most of his bummers returned "each with his own tale of hair-raising escape." However, Belknap's horse, which had carried him "hundreds of miles," was among the day's casualties. He later recalled, "My horse was giving his life to save mine. I could feel his body quiver as deadly bullets struck him." The noble animal reached Union lines before it "dropped on his knees and fell dead."[132]

The Twenty-First Michigan took 230 men into the Battle of Bentonville and suffered 92 casualties (6 officers and 86 enlisted men). One exceptionally fortunate Grand Rapids officer was Lieutenant Robert Wilson, who had entered the service as a nineteen-year-old in August 1862. A bullet struck his brass saber belt buckle but only bruised him. Two other Kent County officers wounded at Bentonville included Lieutenant Amherst B. Cheney and Lieutenant Sanford W. Lyon. A bullet hit Cheney in the chest without hitting a vital organ. He exited the field on his own power and so did Lyon, who was shot in the leg. Both men survived their wounds. After the battle, Captain Prince and his men earned accolades. Division commander General Williams Carlin noted the Michiganians performed "coolly and deliberately," while brigade commander General George P. Buell complimented Prince for his gallant behavior.[133]

Within a few weeks of the Battle of Bentonville, the Civil War ended. Sherman's army, including the Twenty-First Michigan, headed to Washington, D.C. Relieved of any future fighting, the Michiganians set a personal wartime record, covering the 280 miles to Richmond in eight days—averaging an impressive 35 miles per day. The Twenty-First Michigan reached the nation's capital on May 12, and two weeks later, the regiment participated in the Grand Review. The review proved rewarding for Sherman's bummers. While most units, especially those from the eastern armies, looked their best, General Sherman allowed his foragers to swagger "bummer style." According to one, "We marched, or rather walked, down Pennsylvania Avenue, a ragged bunch of tired men." It didn't matter how they looked or marched, an appreciative crowd tossed them cakes and candy.[134]

On June 8, the Twenty-First unceremoniously mustered out of service and boarded a train to Detroit, where the men were paid off and headed home. One postwar veteran of considerable note, Captain Charles E. Belknap, served Grand Rapids in many capacities, most notably as mayor, congressman and historian.[135]

WAR AFFECTS THE VALLEY CITY

*The people of Grand Rapids have shown a spirit and energy
worthy of wide imitation.*
—Detroit Free Press, *August 12, 1862*

The war years brought understandable changes to Grand Rapids, especially as soldiers played a major and varied role in the city's daily activities. Shortly after the Third Michigan Infantry left for the nation's capital, Congressman Francis W. Kellogg arranged for Grand Rapids to be the rendezvous point for two new regiments of cavalry (Second and Third) and two new batteries of artillery (Batteries B and C). In mid-1862, enlistments at the county fairgrounds presented "a busy and inspiring scene throughout the summer," including the mustering of two more regiments of cavalry (Sixth and Seventh). Two years later, "swarms" of soldiers (one estimate placed the number as high as five thousand men) arrived and departed during the early months of 1864. In mid-1864, residents enthusiastically welcomed Third Michigan Infantry veterans returning home at the end of their three-year term of enlistment. The designation of Grand Rapids as the state's draft rendezvous also contributed to a constant flow of troops moving into and out of the city. Camp Lee, named after a U.S. Army officer from Detroit who commanded the post (not the famed Rebel general), opened in late 1863.[136]

Speakers at frequent public meetings held through the war's final weeks encouraged volunteers to fill manpower quotas and avoid the embarrassment of succumbing to the draft. On August 9, 1862, Grand

Thirty-one-year-old Edward S. Nixon of Grand Rapids commanded Company F, Fourteenth Michigan Infantry, a company largely composed of Kent County men. After a slow start in the war, the Fourteenth saw active duty in the Atlanta Campaign, as well as the march through Georgia and the Carolina Campaign. Nixon mustered out in January 1865. *Courtesy of the State Archives of Michigan.*

Rapids hosted a mass meeting of upward of three thousand people on Fulton Street near today's Davenport University. Among the day's speeches, Congressman Kellogg assured prospective enlistees that they were not only "the heroes of to-day, but the heroes of all time," whose names and memories "would be held in the same veneration" as the men who fought and won the American Revolution. According to one observer, "[A]bout one hundred men enlisted that day." Enthusiastic residents also contributed $3,200, with others donating forty acres and two cows to be sold to raise additional dollars for the war effort. The *Detroit Free Press* chronicled, "The people of Grand Rapids have shown a spirit and energy worthy of a wide imitation." Bounty money also encouraged volunteering. In late 1863, the Kent County Board of Supervisors supported giving each volunteer a $200 bonus. In March 1864, the Grand Rapids City Council authorized a $100 bounty. On two occasions in 1864, voters overwhelmingly supported offering these allotments.[137]

WHAT THE SOLDIERS SHARED WITH THOSE BACK HOME

Soldiers' letters published in the local newspapers also allowed folks to share experiences that ranged from enlightening to disturbing.

On January 15, 1862, "Walter" and a fellow buddy from the Third Michigan Infantry visited Mount Vernon, George Washington's home. In a lengthy letter, Walter described seeing several abandoned slave plantations along the way. Their dilapidated condition caused him to contemplate how

Virginia might "suffer many years before she can recover from the shock she has received from this rebellion." At Mount Vernon, an anxious housekeeper feared the Northern visitors might miss seeing a "donations box." (Walter did not indicate if he placed any money in the box.) Inside the house, the men encountered a "badly kept" harpsichord, a broken earthen platter and a few other artifacts allegedly once used by the first president. Walter conceded there was "nothing to admire," except that these items had once "been used by and belonged to the Father of our Country." Despite some apparent disappointment, Walter experienced "a feeling of reveredtial [sic] awe, akin to that awakened when walking in old Rome through the aisles and halls, that once resounded to the tread of the Caesars."[138]

Conversely, Abner M. Cook's letter about the activities of the Eighth Michigan Infantry must have affeccted readers quite differently. In early January 1862, the thirty-seven-year-old Grand Rapids soldier detailed a reconnaissance mission to a nearby abandoned plantation near Beaufort, South Carolina. With no Rebels around, the Yankees stacked their rifles, and with "each man for himself," they headed for the main house. "Not so much after plunder," Cook modestly explained, but to see what they could find to supplement their hardtack. The men confiscated all the foodstuffs ("cream, milk, butter, preserves, blackberry jam, pickles, etc. etc."). Cook and his buddies then moved "in great haste" through the main house, paying "attention to the stands, trunks, boxes, library, etc." They found "abundant evidence everywhere (but especially upstairs in the young ladies' room) of cultivation, education and refinement." Smitten by a wave of humility, Cook added, "Of course, I cannot enter into a detailed account of these things, but will simply say that each one appropriated to himself those things that seemed most pleasing to his own eye." However, Cook faced a "predicament," finding "nothing good enough for me to take except a carpet blanket." The actions of Abner Cook and his comrades confirmed what one Ottawa County soldier later observed, "War makes a person forget his Christian upbringing."[139]

THE "LONG ARM" AND SHARPSHOOTERS

Grand Rapids also served as the organizational home for four of Michigan's fourteen artillery batteries. Mustered on November 26, 1861, Battery B was heavily engaged at the Battle of Shiloh on April 6, 1862, and suffered fifty-two men taken prisoner and lost four of its six guns. The captured men were eventually exchanged and saw service later during the Atlanta Campaign. Battery B also participated in Sherman's March to the Sea, seeing action at the Battle of Griswoldville, where it performed "most excellent service...distinguishing itself by rapid and effective firing." Battery B also participated in the Carolina Campaign. Organized at the same time as Battery B, Battery C entered into Federal service in Grand Rapids on December 17, 1861. It saw action during the Corinth and Iuka (Mississippi) Campaigns during the fall of 1862, as well as the Atlanta and the March to the Sea Campaigns. Battery K left Grand Rapids in June 1863. After a short stay in Washington, D.C., it joined the Army of the Cumberland and spent much of the war garrisoning the Union forts around Chattanooga, Tennessee. After filling the First Michigan Artillery Regiment with twelve batteries, Michigan organized two additional batteries. The Thirteenth Battery was mustered on January 20, 1864, at Grand Rapids and left for Washington, D.C., a few weeks later. Manning the guns at Fort Slemmer, one of the forts protecting the nation's capital, the Michiganians helped repulse the Rebel raid on the capital in July 1864. Later in the war, these gunners received horses and joined missions hunting down Rebel guerrillas and President Lincoln's assassins.[140]

Two other batteries had more solid Grand Rapids connections. Organized in Marshall in late 1861, Battery E was commanded by Captain John H. Dennis of Grand Rapids. Originally a captain in the Third Michigan Infantry, Dennis left service on June 9, 1862. Lieutenant John Ely, also of Grand Rapids, replaced him. Ely mustered out on July 20, 1865, leaving the army as a brevet lieutenant colonel. Battery E spent much of the war in Nashville, Tennessee, and saw considerable action repulsing the Rebel attack on the Tennessee capital in mid-December 1864. A Grand Rapids officer also commanded Battery L. Lieutenant Carlton Neal of Grand Rapids began his military career as a second lieutenant with the Third Michigan Infantry. He transferred to the artillery in late 1862 and, in February 1865, earned the rank of captain. According to an on-the-scenes observer, Captain Neal's battery was "composed of a fine looking body of men, and the neatness and order displayed in personal appearance, and about their quarters, speaks well for the discipline of the commander." To celebrate his promotion, fellow Grand Rapids officers from the nearby camp of the Tenth Michigan Cavalry joined him for a "sumptuous feast." One participant boasted, "We did ample justice to the chicken, turkey, pies, cakes, tarts, etc. and to say nothing of the 'wine that maketh glad the heart of man.'"[141]

During the early weeks of the war, several west Michigan cities, including Grand Rapids, conducted shooting exercises for Hiram Berdan's U.S. Sharpshooters. (A New Yorker, Berdan received permission to form two sharpshooting regiments; companies came from several states.) In one Grand Rapids competition, nine of the thirteen individuals passed the rigid test—despite shooting on a windy day. When the first sharpshooting company was organized, at least two Grand Rapids soldiers served as noncommissioned officers—Third Sergeant James Way and Second Corporal Byron Brewer. In another similar episode, Captain John A. McNeil received Colonel Berdan's permission to raise a Grand Rapids company of sharpshooters. As a recruiting incentive, McNeil offered a "premium bounty" once one hundred sharpshooters had enlisted. After dividing the men into four twenty-five-man squads, a shoot-off would be held—each man getting one shot at forty rods (110 yards). The leader of the winning team received a Grand Rapids lot McNeil owned. The historical record is silent about the property's location, if the competition was held or the prize awarded. As for Captain McNeil, he served in the Sixteenth Michigan Infantry until resigning his commission in May 1862. A few stories in the Grand Rapids press also indicated efforts were being made in late 1863 to enlist men for the First Michigan Colored Infantry Regiment. Once again, the historical record is incomplete.[142]

A FEW GENERALS

Grand Rapids accounted for seven generals during the Civil War. Both Stephen G. Champlin and Byron Root Pierce earned brigadier stars, while five others received brevet (honorary) promotions late in the war.

Stephen Gardner Champlin

A lawyer by trade, Stephen Gardner Champlin arrived in Grand Rapids in 1853 from his native New York. Besides opening a law practice and successfully running for judge and then county prosecutor, Champlin was also elected captain of the Grand Rapid Light Artillery militia company. He later served as major of the Grand River Battalion, composed of several area militia companies. With the outbreak of the Civil War, Champlin mustered into federal service as a major of the Third Michigan Infantry Regiment. In October 1861, he was promoted to colonel—jumping over the regiment's second in command—possibly a reflection of his political connections. Champlin's fellow officers presented him with a fine horse as a New Year's Eve gift, and according to one soldier, "The Colonel is universally popular and will be followed by the boys wherever he leads." On May 31, 1862, Champlin was badly wounded in the hip at the Battle of Fair Oaks. He recuperated in Grand Rapids but returned prematurely to active duty. On August 29, Champlin led the Third Michigan in heavy fighting at the Second Battle of Bull Run. According to Champlin's brigade commander, the colonel's "wounds broke out afresh on the field owing to over-exertion [and left him] completely prostrated." During a second convalescence, Champlin was promoted to brigadier general, but he never returned to active service. In September 1863, Champlin assumed command of the Grand Rapids conscription depot.

Grand Rapids lawyer Stephan G. Champlin entered the service as major of the Third Michigan Infantry in June 1861. Although severely wounded at the Battle of Fair Oaks, he returned to action and led his regiment in heavy fighting at the Battle of Second Bull Run. Champlin earned a promotion to brigadier general but did not survive the war, dying in early 1864. *Courtesy of Grand Rapids Public Library.*

However, consumption (a condition he had contracted in late 1862) soon led him to resign his commission. General Champlin died on January 26, 1864, and was buried in Grand Rapids.[143]

Byron Root Pierce

Byron R. Pierce came to Grand Rapids from his native New York in 1856, opening a dentist's office. Before the war, he commanded the city's most elite militia unit, the Valley City Guards. When the Third Michigan Infantry left Grand Rapids, Pierce commanded Company K.

He enjoyed steady promotions, receiving his appointment as a brigadier general in June 1864. According to a postwar legend, Pierce earned his star after leading his regiment in a charge witnessed by Generals U.S. Grant and Winfield Scott Hancock. As the battle raged, a staff officer approached Pierce with word of his promotion. The colonel asked, "Can you give me the oath of office here? I'd like to die a brigadier general." Stepping behind a tree as bullets whizzed about, Pierce took the oath and then returned to the fight. He later led a brigade that saw extensive action throughout the Petersburg and Appomattox Campaigns. At Sailor's Creek on April 6, 1865, his men captured three hundred enemy wagons, five Rebel flags and "a large number of prisoners," earning him a promotion to brevet major general and recognition "as cool under fire as on parade." After the war, Pierce, who survived five wounds, resumed his Grand Rapids dental practice and held a variety of Grand Army of the Republic offices, including commandant of the Michigan Home for Veterans.[144]

BREVET BRIGADIER GENERALS

Russell Alexander Alger

Twenty-four-year-old Ohio native Russell A. Alger moved to the Valley City in 1860 and married Annette Huldana Squire Henry of Grand Rapids the following year. He began his army career as a private but soon earned a captain's commission in the Second Michigan Cavalry. Alger later served as lieutenant colonel of the Sixth Michigan Cavalry and colonel of the Fifth Michigan Cavalry. He left the service in September 1864 and returned to Michigan, where he earned a fortune as a lumber baron. He entered politics and added elections as governor and U.S. senator to his illustrious public service record. Appointed U.S. secretary of war in 1897 by President William McKinley, Alger orchestrated the nation's military response during the Spanish-American War.[145]
Brevet Brigadier General issued: June 11, 1865.
Brevet Major General issued: June 11, 1865.

William Power Innes

A native New Yorker, William Power Innes started working as engineer at the age of sixteen. He arrived in Michigan in 1853, settling in Grand Rapids. When organizers planned a Michigan engineering regiment, all eyes turned to Innes, who soon commanded the First Michigan Engineers and Mechanics from its inception until his resignation in late 1864. Under Innes's leadership, the Engineers earned a well-deserved reputation. After the war, Innes spent three years in Tennessee managing railroads before returning to Grand Rapids.[146]

Brevet Brigadier General issued: March 13, 1865.

Milton Smith Littlefield

Twenty-year-old Milton Smith Littlefield moved with his parents from New York to Grand Rapids in 1850. The young Littlefield taught school and served in the local militia company before relocating to Jerseyville, Illinois, in 1856. Active in local Republican Party politics, Littlefield was "deeply involved" in campaigning for fellow Illinoisan Abraham Lincoln. At the outbreak of the war, he captained Company F, Fourteenth Illinois Infantry, which saw action at the Battle of Shiloh. Later in the war, Littlefield played an active role in recruiting African Americans for the Union army. During Reconstruction, he lived in North Carolina, earning a dubious reputation for being "involved in an unknown variety and number of schemes…swindling both the state and individuals of millions of dollars." Littlefield's political influence kept him out of jail. The historical record is silent if he ever returned to Grand Rapids.[147]

Brevet Brigadier General issued: November 26, 1864.

Israel Canton Smith

A Grand Rapids native, Israel Canton Smith joined the Third Michigan Infantry as a private shortly after the war began. An officer's commission soon followed, and Smith was often found where the fighting was the fiercest. Twice wounded at the Second Battle of Bull Run, he rallied troops in the Wheatfield at Gettysburg until a wound forced him to leave the field. Smith never returned to the Third Michigan Infantry but enlisted in the Tenth

Michigan Cavalry as a major. By war's end, he commanded the Tenth, earning numerous commendations from his superiors.[148]
Brevet Brigadier General issued: March 13, 1865.

Ambrose A. Stevens

A native New Yorker, twenty-seven-year-old Ambrose A. Stevens arrived in Ionia in 1856. He worked in the mercantile trade and captained the Boston Light Guard, a company formed in western Ionia County. At the outbreak of the war, he was appointed lieutenant colonel of the Third Michigan Infantry, earning accolades after assuming command of the regiment when Colonel Champlin fell wounded at Fair Oaks. Stevens later commanded the Twenty-First Michigan Infantry Regiment and suffered a slight wound at the Battle of Perryville. Plagued by rheumatism and diarrhea, Stevens relinquished regimental command in early 1863. He later commanded in the Veterans' Reserve Corps before overseeing the prisoner-of-war camp in Indianapolis, Indiana. After the war, Stevens settled in Grand Rapids, where he published a newspaper (*Grand Rapids Democrat*) before entering the engraving and printing business.[149]
Brevet Brigadier General issued: March 7, 1865.

POLITICS

The birth of the Republican Party challenged the traditional hold the Democratic Party enjoyed in Grand Rapids and Kent County. In 1854, Kent County voters narrowly supported Republicans (1,540 to 1,493). In Grand Rapids, Republican gubernatorial nominee Kinsley Bingham defeated Democrat John S. Barry by a single vote (375 to 374). Softening the blow of losing Kent County for the first time, the local Democratic press advised the upstart Republicans to "rejoice, hurrah, throw up your caps… laugh at the Democrats, fire the cannon, shout, eat oysters, imbibe, pocket the stakes, and do all other things that victors, may of right do, and we will not complain…[since] the day of rejoicing will soon be at an end." The *Grand Rapids Enquirer* was wrong. In the 1856 presidential election, Kent County favored Republican John C. Frémont over Democrat (and eventual national winner) James C. Buchanan 2,931 to 2,516. In Grand Rapids,

Frémont secured a paltry 4-vote margin (705 to 701). In the gubernatorial race, Grand Rapids voters gave Democrat Alpheus S. Felch a slight edge over Republican incumbent Kinsley Bingham (738 to 704).[150]

Grand Rapids citizens greeted the 1860 presidential election with "a great deal of earnestness and popular enthusiasm," and the Republicans increased their winning margins in both the city and county. In Grand Rapids, Republican Abraham Lincoln overwhelmed Democratic challenger Stephen Douglas 921 to 625, while in Kent County the Republicans enjoyed an equally impressive victory, 3,647 to 2,540. In 1864, Lincoln narrowly lost Grand Rapids to Democratic challenger General George McClellan 813 to 823. Kent County remained loyal to the president (3,398 to 2,966).[151]

The soldiers' vote proved crucial in the 1864 presidential election, with President Lincoln receiving about 78 percent nationally. In Michigan, Lincoln won the soldiers' vote by a three-to-one margin. Kent County soldiers voted for Lincoln by the same margin. Kent County regiments whose votes were recorded (Third Infantry, Seventh and Tenth Cavalry and First Engineers) totaled 1,289 for Lincoln and 456 for McClellan. (No votes were recorded for the Sixth Cavalry or the Twenty-First Infantry.) One Grand Rapids soldier wrongly predicted his regiment unanimously favored "Old Abe." (Instead, the Tenth Cavalry voted 101 to 29 for Lincoln.) However, he accurately forecast a popular sentiment among soldiers: "I won't vote against a Government that I am willing to support with my rifle."[152]

During the war years, Grand Rapids mayors were Democrats (George H. White, 1861–62, and Charles C. Comstock, 1863–64), but in 1865, voters elected Republican Wilder D. Foster. Republicans generally served as state senators or state representatives (men like James Dockeray, John Porter, Augustus D. Griswold and Milton C. Watkins). One exception was Democrat George H. White, who represented Kent County in the Michigan House of Representatives in 1863–64.[153]

CONGRESSMAN FRANCIS WILLIAM KELLOGG

Francis William Kellogg was one of west Michigan's most prominent political figures. Born in Worthington, Massachusetts, in 1810, Kellogg moved to Columbus, Ohio, in 1833. Arriving in Grand Rapids in 1855, he opened the lumbering firm of Kellogg, White & Company. Entering politics, he served one term in the Michigan House (1857–58) before his election to Congress

Born in Massachusetts in 1810, Francis W. Kellogg settled in Grand Rapids in the mid-1850s and entered the lumbering business. After serving in the Michigan House of Representatives (1857–58), Kellogg was elected to Congress, where he served three terms (1859–65). After the war, Kellogg accepted a presidential appointment as an internal revenue collector in Alabama. He served one term as a Republican congressman from Alabama's First District (1868–69) before moving to New York City. Kellogg died in 1879 and was interred in Grand Rapids. *Library of Congress.*

in the fall of 1858. Kellogg served three terms, defeating his Democratic opponent, former Grand Rapids mayor Thomas B. Church, three times.[154]

Kellogg enjoyed some national recognition, and on at least two occasions, he met with President Lincoln. On May 1, 1864, Michigan governor Blair and Congressman Kellogg accompanied the president on a carriage ride in Washington. However, the most famous (or "infamous") meeting occurred a year earlier when Congressman Kellogg took officers from the recently mustered Fifth and Sixth Michigan Cavalry Regiments to the White House. Captain James Kidd of the Sixth Michigan Cavalry recalled the president's "haggard and bent" appearance but remembered "a strikingly handsome man [on whose brow was] the stamp of greatness." After each introduction, Lincoln shook the officer's hand. As the president moved to leave, Congressman Kellogg announced, these men "are 'Wolverines' and are on the track of [Rebel cavalier] Jeb Stuart, whom they propose to pursue and capture." As Kidd later recounted, with "a twinkle of the eye," Lincoln slowly responded, "Gentlemen…I can assure you that it would give me much greater pleasure to see 'Jeb Stuart' in captivity than it has given me to see you." With a bow and smile, the president left the room.[155]

In early May 1863, two thousand women in St. Louis, Missouri, gave Congressman Kellogg a rousing reception. Delivering a speech filled with "confidence and hope," Kellogg denounced the Southern rebellion as "the greatest crime ever committed in all the tide of time." The congressman stressed the North had to win the war since the eyes of the world were on the United States, which represented "the last hope of those who believed in man's capacity to govern himself." Kellogg urged the women "to make their influence felt in every home" until the Stars and Stripes flew once again "in triumph from every hill top on the continent."

Congressman Kellogg also enjoyed the respect of men who volunteered. After the Sixth Michigan Cavalry arrived in the nation's capital, Kellogg received a note describing him as "a constant, generous and patriotic friend" of the regiment's officers. Kellogg's "devoted and unselfish interest in the holy cause…[had] won the heart of every soldier who has ever heard your name." Considering the congressman "a steady and untiring friend," the officers included a gift of $444, describing it as "a trifling expression of our affection for the deserving and faithful patriot."[156]

In 1865, President Andrew Johnson appointed Kellogg collector of internal revenue for Alabama. He was later elected to Congress from that state.[157]

MINISTERS AND DOCTORS WHO SERVED

Among the Grand Rapids professional class, doctors and ministers actively aided the war effort.

Stephen S.N. Greeley ranked among the city's most outspoken and visible ministers. Having arrived in Grand Rapids in 1857, Greeley ministered at the First Congregational Church, one of the city's oldest congregations. In the days immediately following the surrender of Fort Sumter, the Reverend Greeley addressed the Congregational General Association of Michigan, an organization of 130 churches with 7,800 statewide members. Greeley spoke about "a rebellion of gigantic proportions…inaugurated against the Government and the Union of the United States." Attributing the causes "directly and indirectly" to the institution of slavery, Greeley explained the goal of the so-called Southern Confederacy was "the subjugation of the free states." Greeley predicted the "desperate struggle" ahead threatened the "progress of civilization." During the summer of 1862, Greeley joined the Sixth Michigan Cavalry as chaplain. One soldier who served with Father Greeley characterized him as "a powerful pulpit orator, a kind-hearted, simple-minded gentleman of the old school." Throughout the war, Father Greeley's letters from the front appeared in the local press.[158]

Another popular Grand Rapids minister who went to war was the Reverend Dr. Francis H. Cuming. Educated in New Jersey, Cuming settled in Grand Rapids in 1843 and preached at St. Mark's Episcopal Church. "An earnest and impressive preacher," Cuming "at once won recognition as a devoted and energetic church leader." He served the Third Michigan Infantry as chaplain until failing health—a combination of his advanced age (sixty-two) and "the continued exposure" of camp life—forced his resignation shortly after joining the army.[159]

Dr. William H. DeCamp, who enlisted in the First Michigan Engineers and Mechanics in mid-1861, was among the most visible Grand Rapids doctors to go to war. A native New Yorker, Dr. DeCamp graduated from the Medical College of Geneva (New York) and settled in Grand Rapids in 1853. After operating a drugstore for two years, he returned to medicine. As with Father Greeley, DeCamp also shared his experiences from the front with readers of Grand Rapids newspapers. He left the army in October 1864 after his three-year enlistment expired.[160]

The Bliss family sent two doctors to war. Dr. D. Willard Bliss arrived in Grand Rapids from his native New York in 1854. He mustered with the Third Michigan Infantry in May 1861 but left that position in September

Left: New York native Dr. William H. DeCamp, who settled in Grand Rapids in 1857, joined the First Michigan Engineers in late 1861. After three years in the army, DeCamp resumed his medical practice and served as president of the Michigan State Medical Society. *Courtesy of Dave Broene.*

Right: New York native Dr. Charles L. Henderson established his practice in Grand Rapids in 1847. He married Adelaide M. Winsor, daughter of one of the city's pioneer families. In August 1861, Henderson joined the Second Michigan Cavalry as surgeon. A year later, ill health forced him to resign his commission. He returned to Grand Rapids and resumed his practice. *From Baxter,* History of the City of Grand Rapids, Michigan.

1861 and assumed the responsibilities of superintendent at the Armory Square Hospital in Washington, D.C. Renowned poet Walt Whitman, who worked as a nurse in the soldiers' hospitals, maintained Dr. Bliss was the army's "best surgeon." Bliss mustered out of the army in December 1865 as a brevet lieutenant colonel and remained in the nation's capital. On July 2, 1881, Dr. Bliss attended President James A. Garfield, who had been shot by an assassin. Bliss's treatment, however, worsened the president's condition and greatly contributed to his death. Dr. Zenas E. Bliss, Willard's younger brother, also joined the Third Michigan Infantry in May 1861 as assistant surgeon. When his older brother left the regiment, Zenas assumed the duties of surgeon. After the Peninsula Campaign, Bliss worked in a variety of U.S. Army medical administrative jobs until his discharge (and return to Grand Rapids) in February 1866.[161]

New Yorker Charles L. Henderson, who came to Grand Rapids in 1847, mustered in as the surgeon for the Second Michigan Cavalry on August 26,

1861. "Ardent, impulsive and sanguine in temperament," Dr. Henderson resigned in October 1862 because of disability. He returned to Grand Rapids and continued practicing medicine. New Yorker Alonzo Platt came to Grand Rapids in 1842. During the war, he served as surgeon of the enrolling board for his congressional district before returning to private practice "where he was venerated by scores of people, young and old alike." At the outbreak of the war, Lyman A. Brewer, a native New Yorker who practiced in Grand Rapids for seven years, returned to Cleveland (where he had earned his medical degree) and entered the army. Dr. John Brady, a native Irishman who arrived in Grand Rapids in 1860, joined the army in October 1862 as an assistant surgeon, working in several hospitals before joining the Forty-Fifth Illinois Infantry

A native New Yorker, Dr. James F. Grove settled in Grand Rapids in 1856, shortly after graduating from medical school. From August 1862 through June 1864, he served as surgeon with the Third Michigan Infantry. After the army, Dr. Grove resumed his Grand Rapids practice. *Courtesy of Dave Broene.*

Regiment in May 1863. He saw action in the Vicksburg Campaign before returning to Grand Rapids. Jonathan D. Bevier served with the Seventeenth Michigan Infantry as assistant surgeon (June 22, 1862–June 10, 1863), then surgeon, mustering out on June 3, 1865. James F. Grove served as assistant surgeon, then surgeon, with the Third Michigan Infantry (August 1862–June 1864).[162]

George K. Johnson received his medical degree from the Cleveland Medical College and practiced medicine in several Michigan cities before moving to Grand Rapids. Elected mayor in 1859, he resumed his private practice one year later. With the coming of the war, Dr. Johnson joined the First Michigan Cavalry Regiment as surgeon. He saw action in the 1862 Shenandoah Valley Campaign before serving as brigade medical director under General John Buford during the Second Battle of Bull Run. After the Chancellorsville and Gettysburg Campaigns, Dr. Johnson was appointed medical inspector for the Middle Military Department, which stretched from Philadelphia to North Carolina. Leaving that position in October 1865, he returned to Grand Rapids and resumed his practice.[163]

Arriving in Michigan as a teenager from his native New York, George K. Johnson overcame many obstacles in his quest to become a physician. Dr. Johnson joined the First Michigan Cavalry as surgeon in August 1861. Two year later, he moved on to various higher commands. After the war, he resumed his Grand Rapids practice. *From Baxter,* History of the City of Grand Rapids, Michigan.

Possessing a "genial disposition," Samuel R. Wooster settled in Grand Rapids in 1857 after completing his medical degree at Yale College. The forty-one-year-old Wooster entered the Eighth Michigan Infantry as assistant surgeon in September 1861. Later in the war, he served as surgeon of the First Michigan Cavalry, then as Michigan Cavalry Brigade surgeon. Wooster left the army in June 1865 and moved to Muskegon, returning to Grand Rapids in 1871.[164]

Dr. Joseph B. Griswold qualifies as among the most unusual Grand Rapids physicians to go to war. Born in Vermontville, Michigan, he attended Michigan Agricultural College for two years before entering the Second Michigan Cavalry as a bandsman. Receiving a disability discharge a year later, Griswold entered the University of Michigan medical school. Two years later, he left Ann Arbor and joined the Fourth Michigan Infantry Regiment as assistant surgeon. He later moved to surgeon and stayed with the Fourth until it was mustered out of federal service in the spring of 1866.[165]

ECONOMY AND POPULATION

Like many Northern cities, Grand Rapids suffered some economic setbacks at the beginning of the war. Although a local postwar historian boasted Grand Rapids enjoyed "great activity in business circles" by late 1862, in several areas, the numbers suggest a different story. For example, the city's population showed only slight growth during the war years. In 1860, the city recorded 8,090 people; Kent County had 30,743. In the 1864 state census, the numbers showed only slight growth to 8,770 and 33,458, respectively. In 1860, Kent County reported forty-four sawmills producing 25.7 million board feet. By 1864, that number had slipped to thirty-nine mills producing a paltry 12.5 million board feet annually. However, conditions changed considerably during the postwar years. By 1870, the population had increased to 16,508 and 50,410, respectively. Lumbering numbers were equally impressive. By 1870, the county's fifty-seven mills produced 37.3 million board feet annually. During the war years, some of the city's most prominent businessmen were furniture makers Charles C. Comstock, Julius Berkey and George Widdicome, who continued expanding an industry that earned Grand Rapids a postwar international reputation.[166]

One major late-war transportation change occurred when the city introduced a streetcar system that greatly improved travel, especially to the train depot. Service began in May 1865, "a great day [marked] with music, fireworks, speeches, and free rides." A month after the war ended, the *Grand Rapids Eagle* carried a full-page story enumerating the city's many businesses, everything from furniture to bakeries. Grand Rapids citizens were ready to put the war behind them and look to a brighter future.[167]

Memorial and Independence Day Celebrations

Despite the constant distraction of the war, Grand Rapids celebrated special occasions.

On July 9, 1862, Captain John L. Worden, one of the North's early naval heroes, arrived in Grand Rapids. Four months earlier, Worden had commanded the USS *Monitor* in a five-hour epic struggle with the CSS *Virginia* in the first battle of ironclad ships. Still suffering from facial wounds received in the fight, Worden made an impromptu visit to see his mother. Ananias Sr. and Harriet Worden had moved from New York State to Michigan during the 1840s. John Worden did not come west with his parents, having entered the U.S. Navy a decade earlier. That summer evening in 1862, Grand Rapids residents packed Luce Hall for a special ceremony honoring the man responsible for stopping the feared Rebel iron monster at Hampton Roads, Virginia. Program highlights included the singing of three songs written for the occasion. Worden's mother attended the festivities, but two of his brothers were understandably absent. Isaac Worden served aboard the USS *Carondelet* on the Mississippi River, while Lieutenant Colonel Frederick W.

Worden and his Thirteenth Michigan Infantry campaigned in Mississippi. Ultimately, Captain Worden earned the rank of rear admiral and later served as superintendent of the U.S. Naval Academy.[168]

On August 4, 1863, in response to a presidential decree regarding a National Humiliation and Prayer Day, Grand Rapids businesses closed and citizens attended services at local churches. The early September 1864 fall of Atlanta, Georgia, led "a very large crowd" to packed Luce Hall, where Congressman Kellogg's remarks inspired cheers for President Lincoln that "brought down the house," according to the *Grand Rapids Eagle*. The biased *Eagle* added, "'Honest Old Abe' has not lost one whit of his hold upon the popular affection, despite the slanders of his enemies." A few months later, General George Custer and Elizabeth "Libbie" Custer traveled to Grand Rapids to visit her cousin Rebecca Richmond. A gala reception for the famed cavalier fell flat when the train ran late, and most of the citizens had gone home. Although the mayor and the city band welcomed the Custers, no speeches were given and the historical record is silent about the couple's brief stay in the Valley City.[169]

Independence Day always warranted special public recognition, and remembering the nation's birthday took on added importance during the war. On July 4, 1861, citizens erected the city's tallest liberty pole with a long streamer bearing the motto 'The Union, Now and Forever, One and Inseparable." Former mayor Thomas B. Church, an exceptional orator and debater whose son Fred served in the army, shared patriotic thoughts with a large audience. A year later, with the war's success uncertain, the day's subdued events were "tempered with serious apprehensions and forebodings." George Gray, soon to command the Sixth Michigan Cavalry, provided the day's traditional oration. On July 4, 1863, the city was filled with visitors and the day's activities included a balloon ascension, a speech by U.S. Senator Jacob M. Howard and constant thoughts about loved ones who had just experienced the war's greatest battle at Gettysburg, Pennsylvania. The bloodiness of the fighting during the spring and early summer of 1864 may explain why that year's celebration was described as "impromptu." However, a soldiers' fair organized by local ladies raised $200 for the families of indigent soldiers. Commemorating the next Independence Day (July 4, 1865) would be a totally different matter, as Grand Rapids celebrated a hard-won victory.[170]

8

EXPERIENCING THE PECULIAR INSTITUTION

The raising of negro troops goes on & they do nobly in battle. [They] *vie even with the Anglo-Saxon.*
—*Captain John Claude Buchanan, Eighth Michigan Infantry*

When Union armies invaded and occupied the South, most Northern soldiers confronted slavery for the first time. Although most Yankees would go to war convinced that blacks were second-class citizens at best, they often developed an antipathy for the South's "peculiar institution," which they viewed as the war's primary cause. Grand Rapids soldiers shared these feelings with loved ones back home.

In his letters home, John C. Buchanan eloquently expressed a growing hatred for slavery. A Democrat who joined the newly founded Republican Party, the thirty-eight-year-old Buchanan left a thriving dentistry practice to join the Eighth Michigan Volunteer Infantry as a lieutenant in August 1861. Serving in Michigan's "Wandering Regiment" (as it was dubbed), Buchanan witnessed slavery in different parts of the South. In his travels, he became an outspoken critic of slavery and a passionate defender of the Emancipation Proclamation.[171]

When the Eighth Michigan arrived in Annapolis, Maryland, in mid-October 1861, a slave owner visited the camp looking for his runaway slave. Frustrated and unable to find his property, the indignant master started cursing the unsympathetic soldiers. The confrontation intensified, and Buchanan even feared for the man's life. The "well-frightened" man,

Thirty-eight-year-old John C. Buchanan entered the army as a first lieutenant of Company D, Eighth Michigan Infantry, in August 1861. He saw action at the Battle of Secessionville, survived a wound at the Battle of Antietam and rose to captain. After resigning his commission in May 1864, Buchanan returned to Grand Rapids and resumed his career as a dentist. *Courtesy of Central Michigan University Archives.*

according to the lieutenant, abruptly left empty-handed, and Buchanan was certain the slave owner would think "twice" before repeating such a foolish mission.

Two months later, from Beaufort, South Carolina, a disgusted Buchanan condemned "the squalid Poverty & wretchedness of these helpless Beings." He reviled slavery as "a profanity almost unpardonable" and wondered how it had been "endured, countenanced & sustained" by the North. Although pleased slaves flocked to the Union lines, where they found freedom, Buchanan struggled with the dilemma of "what can be done with & for them?" He agonized:

> *The slave Mother presses her child to her Bosom with all the seeming love & tenderness of the enlightened Christian mother but it is beyond her power to develop the Mind of her offspring & thus they live and thus they die. Oh, what an accursed Institution this is, how full of wickedness & cruelty. If there had not existed another sin on this Continent, this is sufficient of itself, to call down the Judgements [sic] of a Just God.*

Despite his pessimism, Buchanan took solace in the belief that slavery's "end is near."

Initially, Buchanan regarded proposals allowing blacks to join the army as dangerous. It "will engender strife & divide the Councils of the nation & may embitter the minds of many who are really Union Men." He feared the slaves' "abject Servility," which he compared to a "whipped Hound," would leave them poor soldiers. He even predicted that fifty masters could "put to flight" an entire one-thousand-man black regiment. By mid-1863, Buchanan reversed his opinion about black soldiers. From Mississippi, he declared, "I have seen Reg[iment]s of Colored men & must confess...they do nobly in battle. [They] vie even with the Anglo-Saxon." He added, "It is a joke upon their masters to lose their property & then have it turn round & fight them."

Other local soldiers expressed similar abolitionist sentiments, confirming for the *Grand Rapids Daily Eagle* that Buchanan's views about slavery were "growing into active life in the army." From the camp of the Twenty-First Michigan Infantry in Murfreesboro, Tennessee, First Lieutenant George W. Woodward of Ottawa County admitted the Union army had changed. "It is now an army of Abolitionists—emphatically so." Woodward declared that "the direct result of seeing the inside of slavery" meant thousands of Northern soldiers would vote Republican when they returned home.

Frederick S. Church, a frequent *Grand Rapids Daily Eagle* contributor serving with an Illinois artillery battery, advised his prominent father (a former Grand Rapids mayor) to "go in heavy" supporting a constitutional amendment "forever" banning slavery. Dramatically promising to "stand by you with my 12-pounder Napoleon," the younger Church admitted he had become an "abolition fanatic." Writing as the war entered its third year, Church admitted "any [Northern] soldier" who could not see slavery as the war's "only cause," should be called "a darn fool." After a year in the South, twenty-two-year-old Private William J. Powell of Grandville noted:

> *When I enlisted, I was not in favor of enlisting negroes, but I have altered my mind in regard to that. I am not so blind as what I can see that the more negroes we have the less white men it needs to whip the secesh [secessionists] provided we can make them (the negroes) fight, and I guess there is no danger but what they will do that without much urging for there are a good many of them here who would be glad of the chance to carry a musket.*

In a lengthy letter that appeared in the *Grand Rapids Eagle*, a Grand Rapids artilleryman rejected the conservative strategy often espoused by Northern Democrats to end the rebellion but leave the nation unchanged (i.e., don't tamper with slavery). The writer condemned those who advocated a "Union as it was," reasoning that this meant "a Union in which the time and attention of Congress and every state legislature in the land shall be consumed in passing resolutions and compromise acts to settle the slavery question." The writer concluded the rebellion had invalidated this position.[172]

Colonel William P. Innes also experienced a major epiphany regarding African Americans. During the spring of 1863, Innes proposed filling vacancies in his First Michigan Engineers and Mechanics Regiment with former slaves. In an understatement, one observer acknowledged Innes, a prewar Democrat whose party was more hostile toward blacks than the Republicans, had made "quite a concession." The writer who shared Innes's plan with folks back home added that the engineering colonel belonged to those Democrats who loved the country more than they did slavery and "are willing to use the negro to put down the rebellion, as the rebels are using 'him to overthrow the Government and destroy the Union.'" (It is unclear if any part of this plan was ever implemented.)[173]

In mid-1864, First Lieutenant Allen Benton Morse, a member of the Twenty-First Michigan Infantry from Ionia, supported a growing radical position that African Americans who served honorably deserved "full citizenship," including the right to vote. Morse argued that a black soldier had "a better right to exercise the elective franchise than the white man who has safely remained at home, and voted steadfastly against every act of the Administration, thereby constantly giving aid and comfort to our enemies." Morse believed the "majority of the soldiers" agreed with him. Black soldiers, the twenty-five-year-old argued,

> *are infinitely better, in every respect, as comrades or men, than those white persons who have stayed persistently at home, and devoted their time, money, and what little talent they possess, in vilifying and maligning every man who has taken a decided stand in favor of the Union and the prosecution of the war.*

Morse claimed he "never" witnessed "any ill-feeling" between white and black troops. Black troops had been hooted at by "stragglers and skulkers," but these critics were "simply cowardly substitutes." He concluded, "Shame upon the man, the soldier, who is willing that the negro should bleed and die for his freedom and ours, yet would deny him the simple boon of manhood." Morse knew what he was talking about; a few months earlier, he had sacrificed an arm in heavy fighting at Missionary Ridge.[174]

Grand Rapids soldiers preferred fighting an aggressive war and supported President Lincoln's January 1, 1863 Emancipation Proclamation, which formally added ending slavery to Northern war goals. Wounded at the Battle of Perryville, Second Lieutenant Albert E. Barr of the Twenty-First Michigan Infantry argued, "We will stand by and uphold the President in any and all measures he may adopt for the speedy suppression of this wicked rebellion," including the Emancipation Proclamation. Critical of "Copperheads" (Northern war critics, most often associated with Democrats), the twenty-two-year-old Grand Rapids officer characterized one Valley City man who supported slavery as "our sworn enemy so long as he holds to such sentiments." A Seventh Michigan Cavalry soldier charged that criticism of the Emancipation Proclamation disheartened and demoralized Union soldiers. On another occasion, Lowell soldiers at the front reacted "with pain and disgust" when they learned that hometown rumors alleged they opposed the Emancipation Proclamation. They vociferously defended their support for Lincoln's aggressive war measures and endorsed the Proclamation as a military necessity for putting down the rebellion.[175]

In early 1863, Brigadier General Stephen G. Champlin shared his thoughts on President Lincoln's use of executive power to end the constitutionally protected institution of slavery. A prewar Grand Rapids lawyer, judge and Kent County prosecutor, Champlin responded to criticism from a fellow Democrat that the president had "abandoned his primary policy of warring to restore the Union." Southerners had not seceded over "infringed rights," Champlain reasoned. Rather, they sought to establish "a slave empire." The general declared, the war had evolved into a conflict of "freedom against slavery." Regardless of whether Lincoln's action was legal or not, "slavery will be swept away like a cobweb." Champlin rejected Northern Democratic suggestions of returning the South to the Union with slavery intact. Opposing the Emancipation Proclamation was "to palsey the President's efforts to put down the rebellion," he warned. Despite opposition from his fellow Kent County Democrats, Champlin's views also appeared in the state's leading Republican newspaper. An understandably delighted *Detroit Daily Advertiser* concluded, "The voice of our Army heroes is too loyal to suit the ears of the Submission Democrats."[176]

Back home, Grand Rapids also expressed its outspoken opposition to slavery. The *Grand Rapids Daily Eagle* circulated a petition favoring a constitutional amendment ending slavery. The newspaper urged residents to let Congress know that as the "sole cause of this murderous war, [slavery] shall at once be swept from every foot of our land." Residents could purchase a twenty-four-by-twenty-eight-inch facsimile of the Emancipation Proclamation for one dollar; disabled soldiers and widows paid fifty cents. In early February 1865, the *Eagle* published the names of Michigan state senators who had opposed ratifying the slavery-ending Thirteenth Amendment. "After four years of war created by slavery for the purpose of destroying the Union," the Republican newspaper railed, "let their names be forever remembered." In the final days of the war, Grand Rapids ladies sponsored a "very pleasant" musical to raise money for freedmen and other refugees. A postwar story about freedmen voting in a Florida town led the *Eagle* to recognize the importance of guaranteeing the former slaves their civil rights. "There can be no peace in this democratic nation," the newspaper argued, "and should be none until every man, irrespective of origin, religion or color, enjoys equal rights before the law."[177]

When possible, Grand Rapids soldiers subverted slavery. During the spring of 1864, Colonel Thaddeus Foote, an experienced veteran who commanded the Tenth Michigan Cavalry, sought to relieve his brigade commander's frustration with "allegedly loyal" Southerners who opposed enlisting former slaves into the Union army. Clearly frustrated with arguments of states' rights and slavery's constitutional protections, Foote sent his men into the eastern Tennessee countryside enlisting black volunteers, who, according to the *Grand Rapids Eagle*, "would rather serve the country and fight for the freedom of their wives and children than to dwell in bondage." The newspaper endorsed the action and concluded the war effort needed "more men of the mind and stamp of character of Col. Foote."

Late in the war, the Reverend Greeley, Sixth Michigan Cavalry chaplain, offered an impromptu address to hundreds of former slaves near Petersburg, Virginia. Delighted to be part of the "grand Army of Liberty," Greeley rejoiced in Congress's recent adoption of the Thirteenth Amendment, ending the "accursed institution of slavery." Greeley welcomed the freedmen, explaining they now had rights other men needed to respect. Rights like "free schools and churches" whose doors would be open "to all classes." However, Greeley cautioned, "In the transition from slavery to freedom, from forced obedience to self-government and self care, you will, perhaps find various perplexities and trials." The battle-hardened veteran optimistically advised the former slaves to "be patient, truthful, honest, industrious, peaceable and law-abiding, and you shall win for yourselves a good report, and the work of your hands in your new manhood shall be crowned with abundant prosperity." At the close of Greeley's remarks, the freedmen "swarmed like bees" to shake his hand.[178]

Certainly not all Grand Rapids solders or citizens favored black soldiers or even the Emancipation Proclamation. The city's Democratic newspaper railed against abolitionism, encumbering emancipation with extreme financial costs or adverse psychological repercussions. The mere talk about abolitionism in the District of Columbia prompted the *Grand Rapids Enquirer* to declare the action would be worth 100,000 more troops to the Confederacy, "prolong the rebellion" and make it "one thousand times more difficult" to suppress the conflict. In the spring of 1862, the Democratic tabloid predicted the Union would "never" be restored if abolitionist tendencies continued to influence government policies and practices. However, most evidence suggests that a large number of Kent County soldiers sympathized with the observation of a Third Michigan Infantry officer. In March 1862, Captain Stephen L. Lowing (Georgetown, Ottawa County) predicted, "The Ark of Liberty…is moving and 'Woe to the man or Party [i.e., Democrats] that shall put forth their hands to stay it.'"[179]

THE HARDER PART OF THE WAR

God grant [that] *we may meet again & be permitted to spend the remainder of our days, at our own fireside, in peace & happiness.*
—*Sophia Buchanan, wife of Captain John Claude Buchanan, Eighth Michigan Infantry*

A paucity of sources makes it challenging to chronicle the role of homefront women during the Civil War. Sophia Buchanan is an exception. The daughter of a Baptist missionary, Sophia Bingham was born in 1831 in Sault Ste. Marie, Michigan, where her father was stationed. In 1854, Sophia married John Claude Buchanan, a Grand Rapids dentist. Deeply religious, Sophia was said to be "spunky, forthright, and charming." Her husband ("Claude" as she called him) served as first lieutenant in Company D (the Grand Rapids company), Eighth Michigan Volunteer Infantry, which went to war in September 1861. Exceptionally literate for the time, Sophia wrote her husband often, and according to historian George Blackburn, her letters "embodied the anxieties and trials suffered by women left behind as the men fought the war."[180]

A year after Claude left Grand Rapids, "loneliness & sadness" caused by their separation led Sophia to recall their last night together. "That beautiful, but to me sad moonlit night [you said]…'Keep up the good courage Sophie…the war will be over soon, & I'll come home all right, in a little while.'" She hoped, "God grant [that] we may meet again & be permitted to spend the remainder of our days, at our own fireside, in peace & happiness."

Sophia remembered the day the Eighth Michigan left Grand Rapids: "As you turned the corner by Squire Moore's, the whole Reg. marching on the double quick, & you ran across the road, to us, gave [our son] Claudie a kiss & hurried on."

Understandably, Sophia's anxiety increased after Claude's regiment saw battle. In June 1862, the Eighth Michigan suffered heavy casualties at the Battle of Secessionville, South Carolina. Captain Benjamin B. Church, Company D commander, was among those who fell. After that battle, Sophia remembered Captain Church and sadly reflected, "Many you marched forth with…are no more among the living." A few days after she penned that letter, the Eighth Michigan saw action in the bloody Battle of Antietam in Maryland. Her husband, recently promoted to captain, was among the wounded. However, he recovered and returned to action.

Sophia abhorred a war caused by the "accursed sin slavery, which is at the root of all our trouble." The South was fighting "to maintain slavery forever & if possible to extend it over the whole land…[as well as reestablish the slave trade] one of the barbarities of the dark ages." Sophia hoped God's "righteous retribution [would] fall upon the heads of those, who have… sown the seed of secession & brought on this most cruel and senseless of wars." Despite being a devout Christian, she "almost willingly" wished her husband could capture Confederate general Stonewall Jackson and "help string him up." Sophia also expressed frustration with the course of the war and some of the North's generals. Following the botched Peninsula Campaign, she wondered, "What do you think of our Gen's, & those who conduct our affairs, especially these last battles; Is it not awful?" In the days following Antietam, the Army of the Potomac's failure to advance led her to ponder, "It does seem strange that our army makes no forward movements." (President Lincoln concurred and fired army commander General George McClellan.) Although expressing "a great horror" about future battles, she understood they were necessary to win the war. She believed McClellan's firing was a good thing

An astute observer, Sophia Buchanan shared homefront anxieties and trials in letters to her husband, John C. Buchanan, an officer in the Eighth Michigan Infantry. *Courtesy of Central Michigan University Archives.*

and reassured her husband: "We out of the army, think it the best thing that could be done." Sophia understood the soldiers' loyalty to Little Mac but hoped that "after a little [time], they will all see [the firing] is for the best."

Back home, Sophia helped organize a June 1863 picnic for departing soldiers. She managed the family's financial affairs, moved in with her parents and raised two young boys, who were "happy, playful & full of mischief as ever." Sophia knitted mittens and shirts for Claude and sent him so many gifts (fruitcake, soap, a bottle of indelible ink so he could mark his clothes) that he asked her to stop the shipments. She ignored his request.

Concerned about Claude's morale, she urged him to write her more frequently. On one occasion, she shared his letter with friends, who listened "with the fullest of interest." Not surprisingly, she sought an invitation to visit. When it did not come, she approached the subject more directly, adding a visit "would do us both good." It did not happen. Sophia also feared the war might leave Claude "a broken down man, in the prime of his life." That also did not happen. In early May 1864, illness led Captain Buchanan to resign his commission. He returned to Sophia and their sons and resumed his successful career as a dentist.

Despite her personal anxieties and troubles, Sophia Buchanan characterized the war as "a matter of life & death, to the most glorious nation, the sun has ever shown upon." Other women in the Valley City shared her feelings.

Several months after the Third Michigan Infantry Regiment departed for the war, the *Grand Rapids Enquirer* expressed a concern that women needed to understand their important role in sustaining the government "by providing for the comfort of the soldiers." Southern women were "the chief support of the rebellion," the newspaper claimed, so Northern women owed "a duty to the country which protects them." The *Enquirer* discounted any concerns that more work might jeopardize their "womanly delicacy." In a somewhat patronizing way, the Democratic tabloid reassured women their "usefulness…will shine brightly and gloriously, even when compared with the greatest efforts of our men." However, the paper also conceded the role of women exceeded the value of "speech making and street corner talk of many of the stay-at-home men."[181]

The *Enquirer* need not have worried. Grand Rapids women actively assisted the war effort in a multitude of ways. Late in the war's first year, they organized an impromptu fundraiser that featured a songfest, various skits and a fashion show of "ancient and modern fashions." The day's highlight was "a pyramid of beauty," consisting of thirty young women seated, one above the other, in the form of a pyramid with a child at the top. On another occasion, when reports reached the city that a local regiment suffered heavy casualties, two hundred women "immediately" prepared articles for the wounded and sick. Their efforts inspired men to raise $900 to fund the purchase of additional supplies. Women also worked to feed Grand Rapids soldiers. On one of several similar occasions, Grand Rapids women provided "an excellent picnic supper" to two hundred members of the Seventh Michigan Cavalry. In a little grove adjoining the city's army camp, tables were filled with an abundance of "good and delicate edibles." The grateful men promised to "gobble up" the Rebels just as they did the food. Each soldier also received a bouquet of flowers. Women provided supplies, especially food, to rehabilitating soldiers. In one instance, the Cascade Ladies Society sent two baskets filled with cakes, pies and other choice edibles to the local army hospital. The *Grand Rapids Eagle* praised the "loyal women" who offered a helping hand to relieve, "as far as possible, the afflicted, and giving courage and strength to the brave men" fighting for the North.[182]

Ladies Aid Societies also raised money to fund activities supporting the soldiers. The Grand Rapids society's 1863 summer festival was one of the "largest, gayest, and most sociable entertainments of its kind" ever held in Grand Rapids. An abundance of national flags and bouquets of fragrant flowers decorated Luce Hall as guests enjoyed delicacies like fresh strawberries and ice cream. One self-described "well-traveled man" offered effusive praise for the Valley City women and their efforts, while another claimed the local Ladies Aid Society was "the best institution in our city."[183]

Soldiers in the field also recognized these efforts. Shortly after the Seventh Michigan Cavalry arrived in Virginia, one cavalier promised his fellow troopers would never "forget the kindness" they had received while training in Grand Rapids. As winter relented in early 1863, a letter from Virginia thanked Grand Rapids women for the "timely" arrival of hospital stores, just as the Sixth Michigan Cavalry suffered much sickness. Chaplain Stephen S. N. Greeley professed, "I know of no ladies who have been more untiring, laborious, and self-denying for the army and for the country through all this war, than the ladies of Grand Rapids." Undoubtedly, Grand Rapids women appreciated Greeley's assessment that they were "helping fight this great battle, and hastening the day of peace and salvation."[184]

Women who did not join an aid society also experienced the conflict and contributed to the war effort. One such woman was Lydia Watkins. Lydia and John Lewis arrived in Michigan from Ohio in 1839, first settling in Clinton County. Following the birth of their third child, Benton, in 1844, the Lewis family moved to Cannon Township, Kent County. Cannonsburg (called "the burg") was about four miles from their farm; a few miles farther north was Laphamville (later renamed Rockford). Three more children were born in Cannonsburg. After John Lewis died in 1853, Lydia married John Watkins, an English native and widower who had lived in Michigan for several years. Two more children were born to the couple. The 1860 census reported a family of eight children, aged two to twenty-two, living on the Watkins's farm. In 1863, nineteen-year-old Benton Lewis joined the Eighth Michigan Cavalry without his mother's knowledge. Their wartime letters reveal a strong-spirited woman who kept the family farm productive during the war while counseling a frequently ill son whose military experience proved less than satisfying.[185]

Shortly after Benton left for service, Lydia offered predictable motherly advice: "I hope you will never allow yourself to be tempted to do wrong such as drinking, swearing, gambling or any of the vices so prevalent in the army." Benton encouraged her not to worry, claiming (possibly tongue-in-cheek) he was "the only person" in his regiment avoiding these vices. Explaining that "not an hour in the day" went by without her thinking about her son, Lydia promised to send Benton "anything you wish." Naturally, she urged him to write often, even scolding him when three weeks passed without receiving a letter.

Lydia also worried after hearing reports that he "was very sick" of being a soldier. Often ill, Benton admitted "a person has to be very careful of himself down here or he will be sick all the time." Lydia must have agonized when her son explained, "We have hard tacks & meat for breakfast meat and hardtack for dinner & hard tacks for supper, sometimes our meat is cooked & sometimes it is not but I don't grumble it is good enough for a soldier." Months after he went to war, she brooded, "I often think of you if you should get killed there among strangers how could we hear from you. I wish you would arrange with some one of your comrads [*sic*] what to do and where to direct to us if anything should happen. I should want to bring you home if I had to come thier [*sic*] myself." However, Lydia likely smiled when her son reported Kentucky girls "made me think of old times, but I tell you they were not Mich girls." Occasionally, a frustrated Lydia reminded him, she had "always" said he "would not answer for a soldier." Despite her son's struggles, she cautioned him about doing anything foolish like deserting. "I would advise you to stay and see it out." Lydia also kept Benton aware of hometown affairs—both the good and the sad. The 1863 Independence Day celebration "at the Rapids" featured a hot air balloon, while the names of several local boys filled the casualty roles after the Battle of Gettysburg.

The Watkins's farm proved generally successful during the war years, receiving "pretty good prices" for their produce. Winter wheat in 1864 "did not amount to much," but Lydia planned to "glut" the Grand Rapids market with cabbages. During the early summer of 1864, the family picked cherries—four bushels per tree. The yield could have been higher, "but the birds are quite a help to us in picking them that we cant reach." To fulfill a Sanitary Commission request, the couple shipped dried fruit to soldiers to combat scurvy.

Lydia was also opinionated. In response to President Lincoln's request that Northern towns devote a day of thanksgiving following the July 1863 battlefield victories, a nearby community planned a lakeside picnic. Lydia supported a day of thanks but criticized the picnic. What "of the thousands that are suffering in the hospitles [sic] from wounds received while fighting these awful battles," she wondered. "I do not feel like making merry," she conceded. Instead, Lydia felt more like asking God "to make short work of [the war] so that our absent ones can return home and then we can rejoice together." She also had political thoughts. As the November 1864 presidential election neared, she reassured Benton that Cannonsburg was voting for Abraham Lincoln's reelection. It was good that it was, since she vowed, "If it did not I would move out of town."

Both Lydia Watkins and Benton Lewis survived the war.

Sometimes women followed their soldier-husbands to war. Captain James Kidd recounted the wives of Colonel George Gray and Lieutenant Colonel Russell Alger "spent much time" in the Washington, D.C. camp of the Sixth Michigan Cavalry during the early weeks of 1863. Mrs. Alger "was a decided favorite in camp, winning the affections of all by her gracious manners and kind heart."[186]

Finally, mothers, wives, sisters and daughters had the grim task of burying their fallen loved ones or helping them recover from their wounds—a role that is usually undocumented and too often overlooked. As the Reverend Greeley observed late in the war, "May God comfort those mothers, wives, and friends whose dear ones will never come home to enjoy these blessings, but whose lives have given them in their purchase."[187]

10

MOSTLY TEARS AND AN OCCASIONAL SMILE

Michigan never sent a braver or nobler youth to the field.
—*Sergeant William E. Thornton, Twenty-First Michigan Infantry, about*
fellow Grand Rapids comrade Private Henry L. Tracy

The untimely and often sudden deaths of local soldiers were among the war's most saddening experiences. One of the city's earliest notable losses occurred following the Battle of Fair Oaks, Virginia, in late May 1862. Heavily involved in its first major battle, the Third Michigan Infantry suffered considerable casualties, including the death of Captain Samuel A. Judd. Described as one of the Valley City's most "universally respected" citizens, Judd was hailed by his regimental commander as "one of the bravest of the brave" and a man whose loss would be "deeply regretted by the regiment." Local firemen also mourned his death, describing Judd as "an excellent citizen, a brave soldier, and a true-hearted fireman, whose noble qualities of head and heart endeared him to all who were fortunate as to know him." Several weeks after the battle, Judd's remains were returned to Grand Rapids. The casket was met at the train depot by "a large concourse" of mourners. As the city's church bells tolled, the subdued procession marched to a local business, where the coffin was temporarily placed. The next afternoon, with city businesses closed, residents attended formal funeral services. Judd's death, the local newspaper eulogized, brought the war—for the first time—"home to our very doors." Sadly, it happened again and again.[188]

In the years of warfare that followed, accounts of soldiers dying—some brief, others more elaborate—brought the distant conflict home to the Valley City. Charles R. Burgess, a two-year veteran of the Third Michigan Infantry who died from wounds received at Gettysburg, left a "desolate hearth-stone," while William J. Slayton, "a most promising lad" and son of one of the city's "oldest and most reliable" citizens, died in Louisville of typhoid fever. The nineteen-year-old member of the Twenty-Fifth Michigan Infantry was buried with military honors, and the *Grand Rapids Eagle* published a letter from a comrade mourning the loss of "one of our best boys."[189]

The *Grand Rapids Eagle* was "painfully shocked" when it learned Lieutenant Charles H. Cary had died of disease in Mississippi. The son of Alfred Cary, a former Grand Rapids official, the twenty-two-year-old Cary served in the Valley City Guards before entering the Third Michigan Infantry as a sergeant major in May 1861. Shortly after arriving in Mississippi, Cary contracted a fever that led to diarrhea. Although he seemed to be improving, he took a sudden turn for the worse and abruptly died. Cary was given a funeral with full military honors, and his grave was "carefully marked with a board" that included his name, rank and regiment.[190]

The war hit one Grand Rapids family particularly hard. Hezekiah B. Smith, among Kent County's oldest and "most esteemed" farmers, lost two sons in a short time. As 1863 ended, the *Grand Rapids Eagle* reported Edgar W. Smith, who had risen in the ranks from private to captain in the Twenty-First Michigan Infantry, died from wounds received at the Battle of Chickamauga. Later in the war, Edgar's brother Erson, who had been captured at Gettysburg, died in Richmond's Libby Prison, described by the local newspaper as "the golgotha [Calvary] of slaveholdingdom."[191]

As campaigning began in earnest during the war's fourth year, the stories of men lost in combat grew more painful. The battlefield death of Captain Benjamin K. Weatherwax shocked Valley City residents. Serving with the Tenth Michigan Cavalry, Weatherwax was killed in an eastern Tennessee skirmish. Weatherwax's commander and fellow Grand Rapids resident, Colonel Thaddeus Foote, described the captain as "always reliable in trying times and one of his ablest and best officers." On May 12, 1864, family and friends paid their final respects at a service held at the First Congregational Church. Following eulogies by the Reverend Dr. J. Morgan Smith and Reverend C.C. Miller, the *Grand Rapids Eagle* reported not "a dry eye" among the mourners. Weatherwax was buried in the Fulton Street Cemetery.[192]

As Grand Rapids buried Captain Weatherwax, the city mourned the loss of Captain Charles "Charley" P. Parks. A father of two children, Parks was "a generous, noble-hearted man, universally esteemed and beloved for his joy in disposition, and [an] honorable character as a man and a citizen." Described as "a good engineer and an ingenious mechanic," Parks served on a Mississippi River gunboat. He was killed when enemy artillery fire raked his boat on Louisiana's Red River. Fellow officers adopted resolutions remembering their friend, whose many qualities included an "ardent attachment to our beloved country."[193]

In the final months of the war, the death of twenty-three-year-old Edward Drew of the Tenth Michigan Cavalry led the *Eagle* to attribute his passing to "the slave-holders' great rebellion." In the same issue that carried news of President Lincoln's assassination, the *Eagle* lamented the death of John McPherson. After completing his three-year enlistment with the Third Michigan Infantry, which included two separate stints in Rebel prisons, the twenty-one-year-old McPherson enlisted in the Twenty-First Michigan Infantry in October 1864. He survived Sherman's march through Georgia and the Carolinas but was killed in action at the Battle of Bentonville on March 19, 1865. McPherson left behind a mother and two siblings. Even after the war ended, the grieving continued. Lieutenant Henry B. Burritt, who joined Captain Church's Eighth Michigan Infantry company in September 1861, arrived in Grand Rapids seeking to recover from a gunshot wound he received only days before the war ended. Burritt's shattered arm was amputated, but he died a few weeks later. A "largely attended" funeral at St. Mark's was "a solemn occasion," as family and friends shed "many tears" mourning the loss of another young man who had died for his country.[194]

Some families suffered in different ways. Twenty-year-old James Hannah enlisted in the Third Michigan Infantry in May 1861. Taken prisoner at the Battle of the Wilderness, Hannah survived seven months in the infamous Rebel prison at Andersonville before his release and return to Grand Rapids. A few months after his capture, his younger brother, John, also serving in the Third Michigan, was killed in fighting at Hatcher's Run, Virginia. Another Hannah brother, nineteen-year-old Alexander, received a disability discharge in late 1864 after being wounded in action serving with the Thirteenth Battery, First Michigan Artillery. As if the Hannah family had not endured enough wartime tragedy, soon after Sergeant Hannah arrived home, his mother died.[195]

Sometimes death sent shockwaves through the ranks. In early 1863, twenty-three-year-old Grand Rapids Sergeant William E. Thornton mourned the loss of Private Henry L. Tracy, also from Grand Rapids. According to Thornton, Tracy was "the life and spirit" of Company B, Twenty-First

Michigan Infantry. During the arduous marches through Kentucky and Tennessee, Tracy helped straggling comrades by carrying their packs and rifles and offering "words of encouragement." Thornton remembered how the men listened to Tracy after supper "with merry songs or anecdotes that would seem, for the time, to carry us back to the happy homes we had left, and forget we were tired, or soldiers." Despite Tracy's youth, he set "a bright example for those who were many years his senior." Thornton concluded, "Michigan never sent a braver or nobler youth to the field."[196]

The sorrow of heartbreaking funerals was balanced with the joy of soldiers returning home after surviving the horrors of Rebel prison camps. Taken prisoner at Charlestown, Virginia, on October 18, 1863, Lieutenant Malcolm M. Moore of the Sixth Michigan Cavalry escaped from a South Carolina prison a year later. According to the *Eagle*, when Moore returned to Grand Rapids in early January 1865, he was glad "to get under the Old Flag again and among civilized people once more." Moore attributed his escape and survival to freedmen, whom he described as "the only loyal people in the slave regions, and much more intelligent, warm-hearted and honorable than the [South's] poor whites." Another Sixth Michigan Cavalry officer, Lieutenant Stephen H. Ballard, endured two years in some of the South's worst prisons before making his escape. Back home, he condemned the Rebels for using "torture, starvation, horrible filth, loathsome disease and lingering death" to kill Union prisoners. George Powers of Third Michigan Infantry was mourned as dead. But he escaped his captors and, traveling at night, successfully reached Union lines at Port Royal, South Carolina, before coming home to Grand Rapids in late 1864. In early 1865, Alfred G. Bates returned to Grand Rapids "for the first time" since heading to war in 1861. Captured at Miner's Run in late 1863, Bates's account of the treatment of Union soldiers in Rebel prisons was "too shocking to repeat."[197]

THE JOY OF VICTORY

The joyful tidings burst upon our people like a thunderbolt, a perfect halo of light and glory.…The streets swarmed with an enthusiastic multitude. Steam whistles, and everything capable of making a noise were sounded, long, loud, and strong, until the city was a perfect Babel of discordant sounds.
—Grand Rapids Daily Eagle, *April 11, 1865*

After months of grim stories about bloody battles, dreadful casualty lists and unrelenting sacrifices, the April 10, 1865 issue of the *Grand Rapids Daily Eagle* celebrated the war's end with a graphic showing an eagle clutching a scroll that read "Union and Liberty" with a headline that cried out "Babylon Has Fallen!" The newspaper hailed the April 9 surrender of General Robert E. Lee's Rebel army at Appomattox Courthouse as a day "that shall glow with universal freedom, and blossom with progress." The night before Lee's capitulation, the nation lay "divided, distracted, bleeding—a giant in battle-harness matched against his brother." Although "still in battle harness," the United States awoke the next day "the greatest, grandest, freest, most powerful Nation of earth." Success for saving the Union belonged to the "kindly, generous, wise, great-hearted" president, who stood that day "at least one hundred feet taller than any other ruler in Christendom." Proclaiming, "Let the bells ring…and the cannon thunder," the Republican daily urged all Valley City citizens to join in the spontaneous celebrations.[198]

News of Lee's surrender spread like wildfire, and soon the Grand Rapids streets "swarmed with an enthusiastic multitude." Steam whistles "and everything else capable of making a noise, were sounded, long, loud, and strong, until the city was a perfect Babel of discordant sounds." Businesses closed, and red, white and blue bunting decorated storefronts, windows and doors. Boys ran through the streets blowing horns and whistles and ringing cowbells and beating drums. By noon, an informal procession of carriages and people on foot paraded through the city "singing and shouting as though the men composing it had brass throats, and an inexhaustible supply of wind." One carriage of twenty veterans of the Third Michigan Infantry Regiment proudly waved their battered battle flags, while another carried a large portrait of President Lincoln. Joyous shouts and fluttering flags greeted the procession as it passed each house. Two area businessmen mocked the Confederacy's inflation-cursed currency by pushing a wheelbarrow with packages marked "Confederate Bonds," which they offered for sale at two cents per one thousand.[199]

Celebrating did not stop when the sun went down. With the city's businesses and private buildings brilliantly illuminated, citizens gathered in front of the Rathburn House. After speeches by various local dignitaries, citizens moved to the Mills & Clancey Hall for a "Grand Union Celebration Dance." Sponsors apologized for the evening's spontaneity and informality but urged ladies to "throw on their bonnets" and celebrate the triumphant occasion.[200]

Woe to anyone who showed the slightest disloyalty, like one "miserable Copperhead" who hurrahed for Confederate president Jefferson Davis. For the man's indiscretion, the *Eagle* approved of "a sound drubbing" he received from a gang of patriotic boys. The newspaper also shamed those citizens (mostly Democrats) who had denounced the Lincoln government and called General Grant a "humbug." Earlier critics who suddenly expressed joy over the North's victory received the greatest contempt. The *Eagle* hoped these detractors would have the future good sense to avoid any "lingering love for slavery, treason and traitors." In an editorial titled "What They Celebrated," the *Eagle*'s editors explained the Monday after Appomattox was a day of "unclouded glory" for those who stood by President Lincoln's policies, most notably the death of slavery and secession and the redemption of the Union.[201]

PRESIDENT LINCOLN'S ASSASSINATION

War-ending euphoria abruptly halted as news about President Lincoln's assassination hit Grand Rapids "like a thunderbolt from a cloudless sky." The Valley City, as in most Northern communities, went into immediate mourning for the beloved leader. After confirming the "dire and irreparable calamity," Mayor Charles C. Comstock ordered flags lowered to half-staff, church bells to toll for three hours and stores and businesses be immediately closed and draped in mourning. Black crape hung on "nearly every door knob in the city [leading] a stranger, not familiar with the cause, to suppose that death had visited every family in it," the *Eagle* mourned. Lincoln was shot on Good Friday and died the next morning. Churches planning Easter Sunday celebrations quickly adjusted their services, with ministers replacing sermons about the Resurrection with "very eloquent and appropriate remarks upon the great National calamity." Parishioners filled the churches to "overflowing." On the national mourning day of April 19, city ministers directed funeral services for the martyred leader at Luce Hall. Grand Rapids residents also supported a national campaign to raise $100,000 (the president's salary had he lived) for his widow. In nearby Lowell, inclement weather drove the solemn services inside a local church, filling it "to overflowing" and leaving hundreds outside in the rain. As the *Eagle* lamented, the "tears and frequent sobs" from the audience "indicated how deeply the people of Lowell loved Abraham Lincoln."[202]

Determining who was responsible for Lincoln's death filled the newspapers with speculation in the days following the assassination. The *Eagle* doubted Southern leaders were at fault. Instead, the staunchly Republican paper blamed Copperheads who had opposed the Lincoln government on most wartime matters. The *Eagle* maintained the disloyal critics had "constantly taught that Abraham Lincoln ought to be shot, hung or otherwise assassinated and his taking would be a praiseworthy and a glorious act." The newspaper thought it was not surprising that "some wretch…so poisoned with venom" would kill the president. However, if the political opposition had expressed itself "in becoming and respectful language," Lincoln would be alive. Instead, the *Eagle* concluded, it was "the copperhead dribble—this black ooze of northern malignity—that poisoned the mind and frenzied the heart of [John Wilkes] Booth and his fellow butchers."[203]

Grand Rapids soldiers at the front also expressed shock and outrage over Lincoln's assassination. One writer reported his brigade shaved the heads of two Illinois soldiers who celebrated the president's death and drummed them out of camp. A Michigan Engineer reported the Union guard around Raleigh, North Carolina, was doubled to contain the wrath of Sherman's men who "swore vengeance." If the outraged, battle-hardened veterans had been "let loose, this people would have wished they never had been born," he speculated.[204]

INDEPENDENCE DAY CELEBRATION

Even the death of a beloved president would not delay the growing sense of joy as veterans returned home from the war. On July 4, 1865, an appreciative Grand Rapids expressed its gratitude to its "boys in blue." The rain and "foreboding clouds" that Independence Day morning gave way to a cool afternoon breeze. The discharge of ceremonial cannon and the ringing of church bells preceded a mid-morning procession that included public officials, war veterans, the city's steam fire engine and up to forty wagons filled with men, women and children. Following opening remarks by Judge S.L. Withey, Byron D. Ball's reading of the Declaration of Independence was among the best "ever heard" in the city. Robert M. Hatfield of Chicago delivered the oration. An abolitionist Methodist minister with New England roots, the Reverend Hatfield earned accolades as "the most eloquent and forcible speaker in the Northwest." One contemporary observer familiar with Hatfield's writings defined his "vim" as "a quality that is a mixture of intense earnestness, manly vigor, logic, directness, pungenace [*sic*] and strength."[205]

As good as the Reverend Hatfield might have been (and the *Eagle* promised citizens "one of the most bold, original and eloquent expositions" ever heard in Grand Rapids), an elaborate feast highlighted the day's festivities. Evergreen arches carrying slogans proclaiming "In God is Our Trust" and "Welcome Soldiers, Michigan, My Michigan" greeted visitors to the Pearl Street Bridge over the Grand River. A line of white linen-covered tables, with seats on both sides, stretched the length of the bridge. The tables were festooned with "numerous bouquets and mammoth vases of fragrant flowers," while a floral display in the center of the table announced "Soldiers, Welcome Home." An estimated 1,500 people, predominantly veterans and their wives, partook of the abundant fare that included roast pig, turkey, chicken, beef, potatoes, vegetables, pies, puddings and ice cream. An evening fireworks display concluded one of the city's most memorable Independence Day celebrations.[206]

In his postwar compilation, State Adjutant General Jonathan Robertson credited Kent County with sending 4,214 men to war—third best after Wayne and Lenawee Counties. Roughly 10 percent died during the war. At least one veteran arrived home with more than war stories to share with family and friends. Lieutenant Oliver N. Taylor, Tenth Michigan Cavalry, reached Grand Rapids in September 1865 with his new bride, "one of the fair Union daughters of Tennessee," according to the *Grand Rapids Eagle*. The newspaper noted the young bride "looks better than" the twenty-eight-year-old veteran, then added sheepishly, "That is not by any means saying that he is not a good looking man."[207]

Those Who Did Not Come
Right Home

Many a muttered curse was heard as we ruminated in the solitude of the
boundless western prairie, upon the fickleness of justice [and] *there was and is a*
bitter feeling among us against the authors of this wild goose chase.
—*Brevet Brigadier General James H. Kidd, Michigan Cavalry Brigade*

Following the Grand Review of the Union armies in Washington in late May 1865, most Northern soldiers headed home. But several of Michigan's longest-serving and most battle-hardened regiments—units with Grand Rapids connections—undertook unanticipated missions that had nothing to do with the original reasons they joined the army. The U.S. government needed a show of force in Texas to convince the French to reconsider their colonizing schemes in Mexico and on the Great Plains to stop hostilities and suppress Native Americans. Volunteer soldiers with unexpired enlistments filled these immediate needs.

Shortly after the original Third Michigan Infantry was disbanded on June 20, 1864, the state reorganized the regiment, which mustered into service at Grand Rapids and departed for Tennessee in late October 1864. In June 1865, the Third left Nashville and traveled by riverboat to New Orleans before crossing the Gulf of Mexico and arriving at the port city of Indianola, Texas. By late September, following "a fatiguing" two-week march, the Michiganians arrived in San Antonio, Texas. They spent the winter in Texas and mustered out of service on May 26, 1866. After marching to the Gulf, the men boarded a steamer to New Orleans, traveling up the Mississippi River to Cairo, Illinois; by rail, they completed their journey to Detroit. During its months in Texas, the Third suffered 156 disease deaths, which the state adjutant general later observed, owed "much to severe marching in Texas, under a hot sun" and camping at "a most unhealthy point, where much disease prevailed, and where the largest portion of deaths occurred." While in Texas, the Michigan infantrymen were joined by the Third Michigan Cavalry, which left Mobile, Alabama, on May 8, 1865, and arrived in San Antonio nearly two months later. The veteran cavalrymen, whose regiment had been organized in Grand Rapids in late 1861, garrisoned at Fort Sam Houston, undertook scouting details as far as the Rio Grande and escorted supply trains. On February 15, 1866, the Third Michigan Cavalry mustered out of service, traveling by boat to Cairo, Illinois, before taking the train to Jackson, Michigan. The thousands of U.S. troops sent to Texas succeeded in their mission. The French abandoned their Mexican schemes, much to the dismay of its handpicked "emperor," Maximilian I, whom Mexican patriots captured and executed.[208]

CAVALIERS WEST!

The Michigan Cavalry Brigade endured an equally demanding challenge. After returning to their camp after absorbing the cheers of thousands of spectators during the Grand Review of victorious Union armies, the Michiganians "immediately" packed and boarded trains, confident they were headed home. The cavaliers were wrong. General U.S. Grant ordered the Michigan brigade west to face an enemy they never enlisted to fight.

When the cavalry train reached Parkersburg, West Virginia, the Michiganians boarded waiting steamboats. Along the way, the prolific Reverend Greeley was impressed with the "loyal people" who stood along the Ohio River shore waving flags. "Our boys harra [sic] till they are hoarse." He predicted "peace, freedom, [and] a glorious future, await us." It was not to be. When the boats failed to stop at Cincinnati the men realized Michigan was not their destination. After leaving the Ohio River, the flotilla turned north on the Mississippi River, stopping at St. Louis, Missouri. Eight days of crowded conditions, poor rations and miserable drinking water that promoted dysentery led Greeley to note that "there seemed to be little care on the part of the managers of the concern, whether the men had any comfort or not." Aware Michigan was not in their immediate future, many men wanted off the boats and officers feared mass desertion. Not to be denied, Seventh Michigan troopers made a break for shore and, in the process, unceremoniously pushed one officer into the river. These troopers were never seen again. With order restored, the brigade sailed to Fort Leavenworth—a 160-mile journey up the Missouri River that took several days. Father Greeley found Leavenworth impressive, but Lieutenant Colonel Kidd sympathized with his men's resentment of being sent to "a hideous dustbowl lacking even the rudiments of polite civilization and which harbored a multitude of threats to one's well-being." Within days of the brigade's arrival at Leavenworth, hundreds of enlisted men had gone AWOL.[209]

The Michigan Cavalry Brigade soon received new orders. The fortunate ones in the Fifth Michigan Cavalry were mustered out and headed home by early July. Many of the remaining troopers faced a campaign into the western Dakota Territory led by a general who vowed the Sioux, Arapaho and Cheyenne needed to be "'hunted like wolves' to extermination." A few Michiganians found the prairie a "delightful country," but most concurred with one Sixth Michigan officer who labeled it the "most worthless country" he had ever seen.[210]

Traveling across the Great Plains, the Michiganians dealt with blinding dust, intense heat, unforgiving thirst during the summer and numbing sleet, snow and cold during the winter that killed horses and left the soldiers vulnerable to Indian marauding. Kidd characterized the operation as a "wild goose chase" and predicted its failure partly because the department "has undoubtedly been mismanaged." He was right. Fortunately, casualties remained low. Some Michiganians viewed their opponents as "a race of brutes" who should be eradicated. Others recognized Native Americans as worthy adversaries. Sergeant Henry Stewart of Wyoming, Michigan, admired the Indians' ability to hit a man at one hundred yards with their arrows. "They ride around you in [a] circle and they will keep their arrows going about as fast as you can shoot a revolver." The cavaliers also admired the Indians' "splendid horsemanship, so easy and graceful in all their actions." Some even expressed sympathy for the Indians. The warriors, one cavalryman accurately concluded, were "not…so much to blame for the present state of affairs" as were white men who broke treaties, trespassed on tribal lands and decimated buffalo herds.[211]

As 1865 ended, some Michiganians headed home. The Michigan Cavalry Brigade was disbanded, and those who remained were consolidated into the First Michigan Veteran Cavalry Regiment. The final discharge occurred on March 10, 1866, at Salt Lake City. As a final indignity, the men's travel stipend proved inadequate, a matter finally resolved by the Michigan congressional delegation who arranged to bring the cavaliers home.[212]

A MATTER OF REMEMBERING

*This monument honors Kent County soldiers "whose valor made it possible for us
to live to-day in this beautiful, peaceful and prosperous city, under the Stars and
Stripes, fitting emblem of a Union of States and a Nation's authority."*
—*Captain Charles W. Watkins, retired*

SOLDIER TURNED ARTIST

Grand Rapids native Frederick Stuart Church achieved considerable fame
after the Civil War. The son of Thomas and Mary Church, Frederick moved
to Chicago before the war, lived with relatives and worked for the American
Express Company. At the outbreak of the war, eighteen-year-old Church
joined the Chicago Light Artillery (Battery A, First Illinois Artillery). During
his three-year enlistment, Church saw action at the Battle of Shiloh and in
the Vicksburg, Chattanooga and Atlanta Campaigns.

His parents shared their son's detailed letters with the *Grand Rapids Daily
Eagle*. During the yearlong Vicksburg Campaign, Church kept Grand
Rapids readers aware of both the successes and setbacks of U.S. Grant's
effort to capture the Mississippi River stronghold. Grant's ambitious
scheme of digging a canal around the city to avoid its mighty guns led
a confident Church to predict the project's success. He was wrong, yet
from a distance of five miles he found Vicksburg "a beautiful little city."

After Grant's army finally isolated the Rebels behind their stout defenses, the month-long, round-the-clock pounding of the city by Yankee guns led to a rather callous observation: "At night it is a splendid sight to look along our lines and over the enemy's position—better than any 4th of July fireworks." After several weeks of the Vicksburg siege, which took its toll and left him twenty pounds lighter, an impatient and weary Church hoped the Rebels would surrender since the campaign was "getting tedious." But he conceded that such an outcome would create "less excitement," since enemy sharpshooters "infuse a little spirit into the boys." Occasionally, Church's wit seeped into his letters. After hard marches under a blistering sun, he hoped to come "across a stream of soft soap and then all would be right—this article being a scarcity just at present." After enduring the mountains of southeastern Tennessee, a philosophical Church also observed, "I am beginning to think more of a mule than I do of a soldier—they do so much for the cause, and so many die doing it."[213]

At the end of his three-year enlistment, Church returned to Chicago. He actively pursued a career as an artist, eventually moving to New York City. Illustrating animals earned Church considerable fame, and he could be found sketching them at both the Barnum and Bailey Circus and the Central Park Zoo. Church's works appeared in prominent American periodicals like *Harper's Weekly*, *Century Magazine*, *Ladies' Home Journal* and *Frank Leslie's Weekly*.[214]

THE KENT COUNTY SOLDIERS' MONUMENT

Excitement filled the Grand Rapids streets on Thursday, September 17, 1885. Hundreds of Civil War veterans jammed into the city—many attending the Army of the Cumberland annual two-day reunion. With hotels overbooked, the city created "Camp Grant" (three hundred tents at the Kent County fairgrounds, as well as four railroad sleeper cars at the Fulton Street siding). Flags and other patriotic paraphernalia decorated businesses and private homes. Two massive evergreen arches stood over Monroe Street at Ottawa and Crescent Avenues. As the *Grand Rapids Eagle* noted, the city was in a "gala mood." For local veterans and residents, the day also marked the dedication of the Kent County Soldiers' Monument. A parade viewed by Governor Russell Alger and Commanding General of the U.S. Army Philip

Dedicated on September 17, 1885, the Grand Rapids Civil War Soldiers' Monument at East Fulton and Division streets earned national recognition from *Scientific American* magazine, which claimed it "surpasses all previous productions of this nature." Made of white bronze (and subsequently nicknamed the "zinc toothpick"), the monument was re-dedicated in 2003 following its restoration. *Author's collection.*

Sheridan preceded the unveiling. According to the festivities' central speaker, Captain Charles W. Watkins, a Grand Rapids veteran of the Sixth and Tenth Michigan Cavalries, the monument honored Kent County soldiers "whose valor made it possible for us to live to-day in this beautiful, peaceful and prosperous city, under the Stars and Stripes, fitting emblem of a Union of States and a Nation's authority."[215]

Portraits of Civil War personalities (including a woman attending to a wounded soldier), various inscriptions, a fountain at the base and a soldier at the top highlighted the thirty-four-foot-tall monument. An 1885 edition of *Scientific American* magazine admired the monument for surpassing "all previous productions of this nature." Local resident Thomas D. Gilbert was credited with raising the necessary funds to complete the project. Gilbert had served as treasurer of an unsuccessful, late-war effort to raise money for a monument. Twenty years later, Gilbert revived this project— once again making a considerable monetary donation. Gilbert also chose the monument's white bronze material, viewed at the time as "virtually indestructible." However, the weathered bronze led future critics to ridicule it as the "zinc toothpick" and charge a "gray" monument dishonored Union veterans. The solution of painting the monument blue worsened the situation. Fortunately, a restoration effort undertaken in 2000 led to the monument's rededication in October 2003.

THE SOLDIERS' HOME

Michigan Civil War veterans coming to Grand Rapids in September 1885 also celebrated their success in getting a state veterans' home built. Two decades after the Civil War ended, Union veterans grew increasingly vocal about the options available to thousands of disabled veterans, many of whom lived in county poorhouses or received care at Grand Army of the Republic veterans' posts. The federal government responded, but demand quickly outstripped the available facilities. An effort to locate a branch of the national veterans' home in Michigan was rejected because similar facilities existed in nearby Milwaukee, Wisconsin, and Dayton, Ohio. Undaunted, Michigan veterans pressed the state legislature, and on June 5, 1885, Governor Russell A. Alger, the former Grand Rapids officer with an impressive Civil War résumé, signed into law the bill creating the Michigan Home for Veterans. Choosing the site for the facility proved challenging. Grand Rapids prevailed, but only after 296 votes in the state legislature. A 132-acre site along the eastern bank of the Grand River, about three miles north of the Grand Rapids business center, was purchased. On January 1, 1887, the three-story building, which offered room for 450 veterans, was dedicated. At the ribbon-cutting ceremony, Governor Alger told the veterans (and an estimated 15,000 people who braved freezing temperatures), "You do not come here as paupers. The great State of Michigan does not name you thus, but in her gratitude that in the hour of our country's peril you, with brave hearts and the vigor of youth, volunteered to face the enemy.…[Michigan] welcomes you here." Demand quickly led to expansion, including the building of a women's dormitory and the opening of an Upper Peninsula veterans' home (D.J. Jacobetti Home) in Marquette in the late 1970s. The 1886 building, called "Old Main," was razed in 1973, but many Civil War veterans rest in the adjacent soldiers' cemetery. Today, the Grand Rapids and Marquette homes, operated by the Michigan Department of Veterans Affairs, can accommodate about 1,000 veterans.[216]

NOTES

Chapter 1

1. *Grand Rapids Enquirer*, April 17, 1861 (hereafter *Enquirer*); Baxter, *History of the City*, 567, 575; *Detroit Free Press*, April 17, 1861 (hereafter *Free Press*).

2. *Enquirer*, April 25, 1861; April 30, 1861; Baxter, *History of the City*, 567, 745.

3. *Enquirer*, April 17, 1861; April 21, 1861.

4. Olson, "Our Pet Regiment," 2.

5. Baxter, *History of the City*, 258, 576; *Detroit Daily Advertiser*, May 20, 1861 (hereafter *Daily Advertiser*); Olson, "Our Pet Regiment," 3–4.

6. Baxter, *History of the City*, 118; *Daily Advertiser*, May 28, 1861.

7. Robertson, *Michigan in the War*, 48–49; *Daily Advertiser*, June 12, 1861; Baxter, *History of the City*, 294–97, 699–700.

8. *Enquirer*, April 23, 1861.

9. Olson, "Our Pet Regiment," 3; *Enquirer*, April 23, 1861; *Daily Advertiser*, June 4, 1861.

10. *Daily Advertiser*, June 4, 1861.

11. Olson, "Our Pet Regiment," 4; *Enquirer*, June 5, 1861; *Free Press*, June 5, 1861; June 6, 1861.

12. Olson, "Our Pet Regiment," 4; *Daily Advertiser*, June 19, 1861; *Enquirer*, May 1, 1861.

13. *Grand Rapids Daily Eagle*, June 13, 1861 (hereafter *Eagle*); *Detroit Daily Tribune*, June 3, 1861 (hereafter *Daily Tribune*); Olson, "Our Pet Regiment," 4–5; Soper, *Glorious Old Third*, 141.

14. Olson, "Our Pet Regiment," 4–5; Baxter, *History of the City*, 576; *Enquirer*, June 15, 1861.

Chapter 2

15. Baxter, *History of the City*, 49–52.
16. Ibid.
17. Ibid., 57, 69–70, 76, 85–86, 89; Fisher, *Grand Rapids*, 114–15.
18. Baxter, *History of the City*, 89, 123–24, 157; Fisher, *Grand Rapids*, 554.
19. Baxter, *History of the City*, 123–25, 173.
20. Ibid., 122, 125; George, *Statistics of the State*, 141, 309.

Chapter 3

21. Olson, "Our Pet Regiment," 5.
22. Robertson, *Michigan in the War*, 51–53; Leavenworth, "Dear Parents," 13–16.
23. Leavenworth, "Dear Parents," 16.
24. Ibid., 17–19.
25. Olson, "Our Pet Regiment," 6; *Enquirer*, July 2, 1862; Soper, *Glorious Old Third*, 178.
26. Soper, *Glorious Old Third*, 198.
27. Soper, Steve, "Men of the 3rd Michigan Infantry," thirdmichigan. blogspot.com; *War of the Rebellion*, vol. 47, part 1, 784–88.
28. *Record of Service*, 3:2.
29. Soper, *Glorious Old Third*, 437–41.
30. Ibid., 442–45.
31. Ibid., 446; *Record of Service*, 3:2.
32. *Record of Service*, 3.
33. *Michigan Medal of Honor*, 32–33.
34. Soper, "Men of the 3rd Michigan Infantry," thirdmichigan.blogspot.com. See also Crotty, *Four Years Campaigning*.

Chapter 4

35. Hastings, "Cavalry Service," 261.
36. McKinney, "Michigan Cavalry," 136; Longacre, *Custer and His Wolverines*, 16–18.
37. Longacre, *Custer and His Wolverines*, 18; *Enquirer*, August 4, 1861; August 7, 1861; Baxter, *History of the City*, 607. On August 13, 1861, the *Detroit Daily Advertiser* reported that Colonel Brodhead accepted a Grand Rapids company for the First Michigan Cavalry commanded by Captain Byron D. Ball. Captain Ball does not appear among officers in Robertson's *Michigan in the War*.

38. Longacre, *Custer and His Wolverines*, 26–31, 36–79, 99–105.

39. Baxter, *History of the City*, 587–88; Thatcher, *Hundred Battles*, 20.

40. Thatcher, *Hundred Battles*, 20.

41. Ibid., 22–26.

42. Ibid., 58–67; Baxter, *History of the City*, 588; Robertson, *Michigan in the War*, 459–60.

43. Robertson, *Michigan in the War*, 473–74.

44. Baxter, *History of the City*, 588; Robertson, *Michigan in the War*, 482.

45. Kidd, *Personal Recollections*, 1–45; Longacre, *Custer and His Wolverines*, 81–86.

46. Kidd, *Personal Recollections*, 51–53; *Eagle*, November 14, 1865; Baxter, *History of the City*, 745.

47. Longacre, *Custer and His Wolverines*, 87–88, Kidd, *Personal Recollections*, 54–55.

48. Longacre, *Custer and His Wolverines*, 88; Kidd, *Personal Recollections*, 48–51, 57–58; Baxter, *History of the City*, 593–94. Poor health drove Elijah Waters from the service in May 1863. He returned to Grand Rapids and, with his brother, founded a successful wood manufacturing operation. Captain Kidd tells of visiting Waters's factory shortly after the war. During that visit, Waters was struck with a new idea on how to make wooden barrels. He secured a patent but did not live to "enjoy the fruits of his invention." Waters died of consumption in 1868 at the age of thirty-eight. However, Waters's invention left his brother a millionaire.

49. Kidd, *Personal Recollections*, 56–62, 67; Baxter, *History of the City*, 286–88.

50. Kidd, *Personal Recollections*, 48; Robertson, *Michigan in the War*, 570; Longacre, *Custer and His Wolverines*, 86; Wittenberg, *One of Custer's Wolverines*, 13.

51. Kidd, *Personal Recollections*, 69–73.

52. Lee, *Personal and Historical Sketches*, 25.

53. Longacre, *Custer and His Wolverines*, 95–96.

54. Isham, *Seventh Michigan Cavalry*, 10–12.

55. Ibid., 12–14.

56. Ibid., 13–14; Kidd, *Personal Recollections*, 73; *Eagle*, February 9, 1863.

57. Longacre, *Custer and His Wolverines*, 99–119; *Eagle*, April 15, 1863; April 25, 1863.

58. Longacre, *Custer and His Wolverines*, 124–26; Kidd, *Personal Recollections*, 111–16; Wittenberg, *Under Custer's Command*, 29–31.

59. Longacre, *Custer and His Wolverines*, 126–27; Kidd, *Personal Recollections*, 120–22.

60. Longacre, *Custer and His Wolverines*, 126–31. Copeland protested his reassignment, but to no avail. He never again held a field command or served with the brigade of cavalry that he had created. Battery M, Second U.S. Artillery (six rifled pieces), was also added to the Michigan brigade.

61. Wittenberg, *Custer's Command*, 31–32; Longacre, *Custer and His Wolverines*, 132–38.

62. Longacre, *Custer and His Wolverines*, 138–42; see also, "Address of General James H. Kidd, at the Dedication of Michigan Monuments Upon the Battle Field of Gettysburg, June 12, 1889," in *At Custer's Side: The Civil War Writings of James Harvey Kidd*, edited by Eric J. Wittenberg.

63. Longacre, *Custer and His Wolverines*, 143–54.

64. Ibid., 153–54; *Eagle*, July 15, 1863.

65. Longacre, *Custer and His Wolverines*, 154–59; *Eagle*, July 15, 1863.

66. Longacre, *Custer and His Wolverines*, 160–65.

67. Ibid., 175–94.

68. *Eagle*, October 29, 1863; Robertson, *Michigan in the War*, 135.

69. Longacre, *Custer and His Wolverines*, 195–205.

70. Ibid., 205–28; Kidd, *Personal Recollections*, 261–317.

71. Longacre, *Custer and His Wolverines*, 228–35; Kidd, *Personal Recollections*, 337–72.

72. Longacre, *Custer and His Wolverines*, 237–53; Kidd, *Personal Recollections*, 373–402.

73. Kidd, *Personal Recollections*, 398–99.

74. Longacre, *Custer and His Wolverines*, 250–64.

75. Ibid., 265–67; *Eagle*, April 4, 1865.

76. Longacre, *Custer and His Wolverines*, 267–78.

77. *Eagle*, April 1, 1864; Trowbridge, *Brief History*, 7–9; Robertson, *Michigan in the War*, 562.

78. Trowbridge, *Brief History*, 10–14; *Eagle*, March 8, 1864; May 10, 1864.

79. Trowbridge, *Brief History*, 24–25.

80. Ibid., 26–27; *Eagle*, February 3, 1865; February 20, 1865. See also *Eagle*, September 28, 1864.

81. Baxter, *History of the City*, 578–583; *Eagle*, January 3, 1865; February 3, 1865

82. Trowbridge, *Brief History*, 32–39, 42; *Eagle*, January 12, 1865; January 15, 1865.

83. *Eagle*, March, 7, 1865.

84. Trowbridge, *Brief History*, 42–43.

85. Baxter, *History of the City*, 571.

86. Beach, *First New York*, 16–22, 44–46; *Enquirer*, August 7, 1861; *Detroit Daily Advertiser*, September 2, 1861; See *Record of Service*, 45:127–36. First Lieutenant Henry W. Granger and Second Lieutenant Franklin G. Martindale joined Captain Norton in Company K.

87. Beach, *First New York*, 40–41, 537–544.

88. Ibid., 269–70.

89. Ibid., 465, 565, 511.

Chapter 5

90. Sligh, *History of the Services*, 7; Hoffman, *My Brave Mechanics*, 4.

91. Sligh, *History of the Services*, 7; Hoffman, *My Brave Mechanics*, 3–6; Baxter, *History of the City*, 586–88.

92. Sligh, *History of the Services*, p. 8; Baxter, *History of the City*, 702.

93. Hoffman, *My Brace Mechanics*, 16–17.

94. Sligh, *History of the Services* 8–10; Hoffman, *My Brave Mechanics*, 29–31.

95. *Detroit Free Press*, October 11, 1861.

96. Sligh, *History of the Services*, 8; Hoffman, *My Brave Mechanics*, 25–26; Dunker, "Rendering Invaluable Service," 39–40.

97. Hoffman, *My Brave Mechanics*, 23–25; Dunker, "Rendering Invaluable Service," 40.

98. Hoffman, *My Brave Mechanics*, 39–42.

99. Ibid., 64–69; Dunker, "Rendering Invaluable Service," 10; Robertson, *Michigan in the War*, 495.

100. Hoffman, *My Brave Mechanics*, 98–110.

101. Dunker, "Rendering Invaluable Service," 41.

102. Hoffman, *My Brave Mechanics*, 122–33; Sligh, *History of the Services*, 16; McKinney, "First Regiment," *Michigan Quarterly*, 144; Dunker, "Rendering Invaluable Service," 41.

103. Hoffman, *My Brave Mechanics*, 149–57; Sligh, *History of the Services*, 18; McKinney, "First Regiment," 147.

104. Hoffman, *My Brave Mechanics*, 155.

105. Ibid., 148–49, 169–71, 179–81.

106. Ibid., 180–82; Dunker, "Rendering Invaluable Service," 42–43; Sligh, *History of the Services*, 20; McKinney, "First Regiment," 146–49.

107. Hoffman, *My Brave Mechanics*, 183–84; Dunker, "Rendering Invaluable Service," 43; McKinney, "First Regiment," 147–50; *War of the Rebellion*, 31:1–68, 78; McDonough, *Chattanooga*.

108. Dunker, "Rendering Invaluable Service," 45.

109. Hoffman, *My Brave Mechanics*, 172–74; Sligh, *History of the Services*, 18.

110. Hoffman, *My Brave Mechanics*, 225–29; Sligh, *History of the Services*, 24; Baxter, *History of the City*, 587.

111. Sligh, *History of the Services*, 22, 26–32; Dunker, "Rendering Invaluable Service," 44–45; Hoffman, *My Brave Mechanics*, 238–55.

112. Hoffman, *My Brave Mechanics*, 278–87; Sligh, *History of the Services*, 32–40.

113. Hoffman, *My Brave Mechanics*, 292–97, 305.

Chapter 6

114. Genco, *Into the Tornado*, 19–21, 25; Baxter, *History of the City*, 456; Robere, "Captain Charles E. Belknap," www.21stmichigan.us/belknap.htm.

115. Genco, *Into the Tornado*, 23–26.

116. Ibid., 34–38.

117. Ibid., 60.

118. Ibid., 64–68.

119. Ibid., 69–78.

120. Ibid., 85–86.

121. Ibid., 102–3.

122. Ibid., 104–5, 108.

123. Ibid., 182.

124. Ibid., 184–94.

125. Ibid., 195.

126. Ibid., 197.

127. Ibid., 281.

128. Ibid., 283–85; Belknap, *Recollections of a Bummer*, 3–6, 10; Belknap, *Bentonville*, 3–4.

129. Genco, *Into the Tornado*, 319; Belknap, *Recollections of a Bummer*, 8–10.

130. Belknap, "Christmas Day Near Savannah," 590–96.

131. Ibid., 327–39.

132. Genco, *Into the Tornado*, 339–42; Belknap, *Bentonville*, 9–10.

133. Genco, *Into the Tornado*, 342.

134. Ibid., 346–56.

135. Ibid., 356–57; Charles Belknap had a rich postwar public life. A year after the war, he married Chloe M. Caswell of Grand Rapids. Besides establishing a wagon manufacturing company (whose "logging truck" greatly aided west Michigan loggers), he helped reorganize the Grand Rapids Fire Department. Belknap served one term as mayor before his election to Congress in 1888. He was reelected in 1890 and 1892, but a dispute over the electoral returns led to a recount, and ultimately, the seat went to his Democratic opponent. Belknap was actively involved in GAR activities, served as the Army of the Cumberland historian and authored the official history of Michigan's role at the Battles of Chickamauga and Chattanooga. Belknap also remained active in local military matters during the Spanish-American War and World War I. "Historical Notes," *Michigan History Magazine* 13 (1929): 364–68.

Chapter 7

136. Baxter, *History of the City*, 125–26; *Eagle*, September 15, 1863; October 12, 1863; *Detroit Daily Advertiser*, June 25, 1863; *Detroit Free Press*, September 1, 1863. For additional information on the Camp Lee controversy, see *Eagle*, December 12, 1863; February 29, 1864; March 4, 1864; March 5, 1864; March 7, 1864; March 11, 1864; March 24, 1864.

137. *Eagle*, September 15, 1863; December 17, 1863; December 18, 1863; December 22, 1863; January 3, 1865; January 6, 1865; January 7, 1865; Baxter, *History of the City*, 125–26, 158; *Detroit Free Press*, August, 12,1862. See also *Eagle*, February 15, 1865; February 22, 1865; Olson, "Our Pet Regiment," 18.

138. *Enquirer*, January 15, 1862.

139. Ibid., January 29, 1862; Rosentreter, "For the Glory," 11.

140. Robertson, *Michigan in the War*, 348–54, 365–66, 68–69.

141. Ibid., 65, 77, 355–56; *Eagle*, March 7, 1865; April 4, 1865.

142. Robertson, *Michigan in the War*, 1461 *Detroit Free Press*, September 13, 1861; *Enquirer*, July 28, 1861; August 7, 1861; *Detroit Daily Advertiser*, July 19, 1861; July 20, 1861; August 26, 1861. For First Michigan Colored recruiting see *Eagle*, December 12, 1863.

143. Warner, *Generals in Blue*, 370–71.

144. Ibid., 78–79.

145. Hunt and Brown, *Brevet Brigadier Generals*, 10.

146. Baxter, *History of the City*, 586–87; Hunt and Brown, *Brevet Brigadier Generals*, 308.

147. Hunt and Brown, *Brevet Brigadier Generals*, 361; On March 18, 1865, the *Grand Rapids Daily Eagle* carried a front-page story about General Littlefield's role in the capture of Charleston, South Carolina.

148. Hunt and Brown, *Brevet Brigadier Generals*, 567; Baxter, *History of the City*, 579–83.

149. Hunt and Brown, *Brevet Brigadier Generals*, 329, 586. Colonel James Kidd of Ionia also received a brevet brigadier general recognition, dated March 13, 1865.

150. Baxter, *History of the City*, 196–97.

151. Ibid., 196–97; Fisher, *Grand Rapids*, 338–39.

152. *Eagle*, June 25, 1864; Robertson, *Michigan in the War*, 76–77. A letter from Jim Saxton claimed Lincoln won the vote in the Twenty-First Michigan Infantry 250 to 150, but that vote did not appear in Robertson, *Michigan in the War*. See *Eagle*, January 5, 1865.

153. Baxter, *History of the City*, 197; Fisher, *Grand Rapids*, 344–45, 354.

154. Fisher, *Grand Rapids*, 353.

155. Kidd, *Personal Recollections*, 75–76; May, *Michigan and the Civil War*, 57.

156. *Detroit Advertiser and Tribune*, May 8, 1863.

157. Fisher, *Grand Rapids*, 343.

158. Kidd, *Personal Recollections*, 56. See *Eagle*, April 4, 1865; June 3, 1865. Greeley's name is also spelled "Greely."

159. Fisher, *Grand Rapids*, 378–79; Baxter, *History of the City*, 296–97.

160. Baxter, *History of the City*, 424, 702–3. See *Eagle*, March 24, 1864.

161. Ibid., 699–700; Fisher, *Grand Rapids*, 423, 428. For more on Dr. Bliss's controversial treatment in dealing with a wounded President Garfield see "The Death of President Garfield, 1881," Eyewitness to History, eyewitnesstohistory.com. See also "Traveling with the Wounded: Walt Whitman and Washington's Civil War Hospitals," by Martin G. Murray, at http://whitmanarchive.org/criticism/current/anc.00156.html.

162. Baxter, *History of the City*, 706, 711–12; Fisher, *Grand Rapids*, 421–22, 426.

163. Baxter, *History of the City*, 603, 606, 708; Fisher, *Grand Rapids*, 425; Robertson, *Michigan in the War*, 25, 96.

164. Baxter, *History of the City*, 715–16; Fisher, *Grand Rapids*, 426.

165. Baxter, *History of the City*, 705; Fisher, *Grand Rapids*, 429; Robertson, *Michigan in the War*, 75.

166. Baxter, *History of the City*, 125; George, *Statistics of the State*, 49, 146, 270 277, 418–19.

167. Fisher, *Grand Rapids*, 555; *Eagle*, May 12, 1865.

168. Beld, *Grand Times*, 63–65.

169. Baxter, *History of the City*, 126, *Eagle*, September 5, 1864; January 25, 1865; January 26, 1865.

170. Baxter, *History of the City*, 126, 167, 169; *Detroit Daily Advertiser*, July 10, 1863.

Chapter 8

171. Blackburn, "Negro as Viewed," 75–84.

172. *Eagle*, June 13, 1863; December 24, 1863; June 19, 1863; March 18, 1864

173. Ibid., May 18, 1863.

174. Ibid., July 23, 1864.

175. Ibid., March 12, 1863; March 17, 1863; April 16, 1863; April 28, 1863.

176. "Stephen Gardner Champlin," Men of the 3rd Michigan Infantry, March 18, 2018, thirdmichigan.blogspot.com/search?q=Stephen+Gardner+Champlin.

177. Ibid., December 4, 1863; December 12, 1863; February 6, 1865; April 5, 1865; June 9, 1865.

178. *Eagle*, May 9, 1864; April 5, 1865.
179. Soper, *Glorious Old Third*, 202; *Enquirer*, May 15, 1861; February 5, 1862; April 2, 1862; April 23, 1862.

Chapter 9

180. Blackburn, "Letters from the Front," 53–67.
181. *Enquirer*, December 18, 1861.
182. *Detroit Daily Advertiser*, December 4, 1861; *Detroit Free Press*, June 12, 1862; *Eagle*, June 23, 1863; December 27, 1864; November 21, 1863. See similar stories in *Eagle*, June 20, 1863; June 22, 1863; October 29, 1863; December 27, 1864.
183. *Eagle*, June 20, 1863; June 22, 1863. See similar stories in *Eagle*, September 12, 1864; January 30, 1865.
184. Ibid., April 16, 1863; June 13, 1863.
185. Everham, "Letters from Home," 35–63.
186. Kidd, *Personal Recollections*, 84.
187. *Eagle*, June 3, 1865.

Chapter 10

188. Robertson, *Michigan in the War*, 53–54; *Enquirer*, June 27, 1862; July 2, 1862.
189. *Eagle*, August 15, 1863; October 20, 1863.
190. Ibid., July 30–31, 1863.
191. Ibid., December 22, 1863.
192. Ibid., May 13, 1864; Trowbridge, *Brief History*, 13–14.
193. *Eagle*, May 11, 1864.
194. Ibid., February 20, 1865; February 22, 1865; May 11, 1864; April 13, 1865; April 15, 1865; May 27, 1865.
195. Ibid., February 9, 1865.
196. Ibid., February 24, 1863; April 15, 1865.
197. Ibid., January 29, 1865; March 21, 1865; October 27, 1864; February 3, 1865.

Chapter 11

198. Ibid., April 10, 1865.
199. Ibid; Baxter, *History of the City*, 274.
200. *Eagle*, April 11, 1865.

201. Ibid., April 12, 1865.
202. Ibid., April 15, 1865; April 17, 1865; April 20, 1865; May 26, 1865.
203. Ibid., April 18, 1865.
204. Ibid., May 18, 1865.
205. Ibid., May 30, 1865; June 20, 1865; July 3, 1865; July 5, 1865; July 27, 1865.
206. Ibid.
207. *Eagle*, September 15, 1865; Robertson, *Michigan in the War*, 63.

Chapter 12

208. Robertson, *Michigan in the War*, 60, 61, 637; *Eagle*, August 28, 1865.
209. Longacre, *Custer and His Wolverines*, 279–83; *Eagle*, June 3, 1865.
210. Longacre, *Custer and His Wolverines*, 283–91.
211. Ibid., 292–93. Irish immigrant Captain John C. Molly and his parents lived in Grand Rapids. Molly started his military career with an Illinois infantry regiment, with which he was wounded. He enlisted in the Sixth Michigan Cavalry in September 1862 and suffered another wound. He was described as "a gallant and brave soldier, an excellent, faithful and competent officer, always at his post, and in front." Molly was killed in action in the Utah Territory. *Grand Rapids Democrat*, February 28, 1866.
212. Longacre, *Custer and His Wolverines*, 293–94.

Chapter 13

213. *Eagle*, February 9, 1863; June 20, 1863; June 27, 1863; December 12, 1863; December 24, 1863; June 7, 1864.
214. frederickstuartchurch.com.
215. Petz and Rosentreter, *Seeking Lincoln in Michigan*, 25.
216. Baxter, *History of the City*, 366–69.

BIBLIOGRAPHY

Books

Baxter, Albert. *History of the City of Grand Rapids, Michigan*. New York: Munsell & Company, 1891.

Beach, William Harrison. *The First New York (Lincoln) Cavalry from April 19, 1861, to July 7, 1865*. N.p.: Forgotten Books, 2015.

Beeson, Lewis, ed. *Congregationalism, Slavery and the Civil War*. Lansing: Michigan Civil War Centennial Observance Commission, 1966.

————. *The Methodist Episcopal Church in Michigan During the Civil War*. Lansing: Michigan Civil War Centennial Observance Commission, 1966.

Beld, Gordon G. *Grand Times in Grand Rapids: Pieces of Furniture City History*. Charleston, SC: The History Press, 2012.

Belknap, Charles E. *Bentonville: What A Bummer Knows About It*. Washington, D.C.: Military Order of the Loyal Legion of the United States, 1893.

————. *History of the Michigan Organizations at Chickamauga, Chattanooga and Missionary Ridge*, 2nd ed. Lansing, MI: Robert Smith Printing, 1899.

————. *Recollections of a Bummer*. Washington, D.C.: Military Order of the Loyal Legion of the United States, 1898).

Cozzens, Peter. *The Shipwreck of Their Hopes: The Battles for Chattanooga*. Urbana: University of Illinois Press, 1994.

Crotty, D.G. *Four Years Campaigning in the Army of the Potomac*. Grand Rapids, MI: Dygert Brothers and Company, 1874.

Dilley, Thomas R. *Grand Rapids in Stereographs, 1860–1900.* Charleston, SC: Arcadia Publishing, 2007.

Everham, Virginia, ed. "Letters from Home." In *Michigan Women in the Civil War,* 35–63. Lansing: Michigan Civil War Centennial Observance Commission, 1966.

Fisher, Ernest B., ed. *Grand Rapids and Kent County, Michigan.* Chicago: Robert O. Law Company, 1918.

Genco, James. *Into the Tornado of War: A History of the Twenty-First Michigan Infantry in the Civil War.* Bloomington, IN: Abbott Press, 2012.

George, W.S. *Statistics of the State of Michigan, Census of 1860.* Lansing, MI: State Printers, 1861.

Hoffman, Mark. *"My Brave Mechanics": The First Michigan Engineers and Their Civil War.* Detroit, MI: Wayne State University Press, 2007.

Hunt, Roger D., and Jack R. Brown. *Brevet Brigadier Generals in Blue.* Gaithersburg, MD: Olde Soldiers Books, 1990.

Isham, Asa B. *Seventh Michigan Cavalry of Custer's Wolverine Brigade,* 2nd ed. Huntington, WV: Blue Acorn Press, 2000.

Kidd, James H. *Personal Recollections of a Cavalryman,* 2nd ed. Grand Rapids, MI: Black Letter Press, 1969.

Lee, William O., comp. *Personal and Historical Sketches and Facial History of and by the Members of the Seventh Regiment Michigan Volunteer Cavalry, 1862–1865.* Detroit: Seventh Michigan Cavalry Association, 1902.

Longacre, Edward G. *Custer and His Wolverines: The Michigan Cavalry Brigade, 1861–1865.* Conshohocken, PA: Combined Publishing, 1997.

May, George. *Michigan and the Civil War Years, 1860–1866: A Wartime Chronicle.* Lansing: Michigan Civil War Centennial Observance Commission, 1966.

McDonough, James Lee. *Chattanooga: A Death Grip on the Confederacy.* Knoxville: University of Tennessee Press, 1984.

Michigan Medal of Honor Winners in the Civil War. Lansing: Michigan Civil War Centennial Observance Commission, 1966.

Michigan Soldiers and Sailors Alphabetical Index. Lansing, MI: Wynkoop, Hallenbeck, Crawford Company, 1915.

Petz, Weldon E., and Roger L. Rosentreter. *Seeking Lincoln in Michigan: A Remembrance Trail.* Lansing: Michigan History Magazine, 2009.

Record of Service of Michigan Volunteers in the Civil War, 1861–1865. 45 vols. Kalamazoo, MI: Ihling Brothers, n.d.

Robertson, Jonathan, comp. *Michigan in the War.* Lansing, MI: W.S. George & Company, 1880.

Sligh, Charles R. *History of the Services of the First Regiment Michigan Engineers and Mechanics During the Civil War, 1861–1865.* Grand Rapids, MI, 1921.

Soper, Steven. *The "Glorious Old Third": A History of the Third Michigan Infantry, 1855–1927.* Old Third Publishing, 2007.

Sword, Wiley. *Mountains Touched With Fire: Chattanooga Besieged, 1863.* New York: St. Martin's Press, 1995.

Thatcher, Marshall P. *A Hundred Battles in the West: St. Louis to Atlanta, 1861–65: The Second Michigan Cavalry.* Detroit, MI: 1884.

Trowbridge, Luther S. *A Brief History of the Tenth Michigan Cavalry.* Detroit, MI: Friesema Brothers Publishing, 1908.

Warner, Ezra J. *Generals in Blue.* Baton Rouge: Louisiana University Press, 1964.

War of the Rebellion: Official Records of the Union and Confederate Armies. Washington: Government Printing Office, 1880–1900.

Wittenberg, Eric J. *At Custer's Side: The Civil War Writings of James Harvey Kidd.* Kent, OH: Kent State University Press, 2001.

———, ed. *One of Custer's Wolverines: The Civil War Letters of Brevet Brigadier General James H. Kidd, 6th Michigan Cavalry.* Kent, OH: Kent State University Press, 2000.

———. *Under Custer's Command: The Civil War Journal of James Henry Avery.* Washington, D.C.: Brassey's, 2000.

Articles

Belknap, Charles E. "Christmas Day Near Savannah in Wartime." *Michigan History Magazine* 6 (1922): 591–96.

Blackburn, George M., ed. "Letters from the Front: A Distaff View of the Civil War." *Michigan History Magazine* 49: 53–67.

———. "The Negro as Viewed by a Michigan Civil War Soldier: Letters of John C. Buchanan." *Michigan History Magazine* 47: 75–84.

"The Death of President Garfield, 1881." EyeWitness to History. 1999. www.eyewitnesstohistory.com/gar.htm.

Dunker, Steven. "Rendering Invaluable Service." *Michigan History Magazine* (January/February 1992): 38–45.

Hastings, S.H. "The Cavalry Service, and Recollections of the Late War," *Western Magazine of History,* volume 11, number 3, p. 261.

"Historical Notes." *Michigan History Magazine* 13 (1929): 364–68.

Leavenworth, Paul. "Dear Parents: The Civil War Letters of George W. Miller." *Grand River Valley History* 10, no. 2 (September 1992): 13–19.

McKinney, Francis F. "The First Regiment of Michigan Engineers and Mechanics." *Michigan Quarterly* 62 (1955–56): 140–50.

———. "Michigan Cavalry in the Civil War." *Michigan Quarterly* 64 (1957–58): 136–46.

Olson, Gordon, L. "'Our Pet Regiment Has Departed': The Civil War Diaries of Rebecca Richmond." *Grand River Valley History* 18 (2001).

Robere, Bruce. "Captain Charles E. Belknap." 21st Michigan Volunteer Infantry. Last modified January 18, 2010. http://www.21stmichigan.us/belknap.htm.

Rosentreter, Roger L. "For the Glory of Peninsula State." In *Michigan and the Civil War*, 9–13. Lansing: Michigan History Magazine, 1999.

Tropf, Jonathan. "Win or Go Home? Michigan Soldiers' View of the 1864 Presidential Election." Eastern Michigan University, unpublished ms., 2012.

Vander Wall, Douglas, and Dr. Marie Heyda. "In Honor of the Soldiers from Kent County, 1861–1865." *Grand River Valley Review* 1, no. 1 (Fall 1979): 30–33.

Newspapers

Grand Rapids Daily Eagle
Grand Rapids Enquirer
Detroit Advertiser and Tribune
Detroit Free Press

ABOUT THE AUTHOR

A native Michiganian, Roger L. Rosentreter is an assistant professor in the Department of History at Michigan State University. He also served as editor of *Michigan History Magazine* from 1988 through 2009. He has written and published extensively on Michigan's past, including his most recent book, *Michigan: A History of Explorers, Entrepreneurs & Everyday People,* published by the University of Michigan Press. Dr. Rosentreter has given numerous presentations on Michigan history with a special focus on the state's role in the Civil War.